NORWICH MURDERS

Norwich City Police, believed to be 1890. Police Archive

NORWICH MURDERS

MAURICE MORSON

Wharncliffe Books

Other sins only speak; murder shrieks out

John Webster (1580–1625)
English dramatist

To all the victims

First Published in Great Britain in 2006 by
Pen & Sword Wharncliffe Books
an imprint of
Pen & Sword Books Ltd
47 Church Street
Barnsley
South Yorkshire
S70 2AS

Copyright © Maurice Morson 2006

ISBN: 1845630025

Typeset in 10/12pt Ehrhardt by Concept, Huddersfield.

Printed and bound in England by
CPI UK.

Pen and Sword Books Ltd incorporates the Imprints of Pen & Sword Aviation, Pen & Sword Maritime, Pen & Sword Military, Wharncliffe Books, Pen & Sword Select, Pen and Sword Military Classics and Leo Cooper.

For a complete list of Pen & Sword titles please contact
PEN & SWORD BOOKS LIMITED
47 Church Street
Barnsley
South Yorkshire
S70 2AS
England
E-mail: enquiries@pen-and-sword.co.uk
Website: www.pen-and-sword.co.uk

Contents

A Norwich policeman in about 1900.

Acknowledgements

I am grateful to all who assisted in the compilation of this book, in whatever role, whether named below or not.

My thanks go to the Chief Constable of the Norfolk Constabulary for permission to research and record from police files. Several retired and serving officers of the old city and county forces gave up their time and memories while the Norfolk Constabulary archivists searched and found and confirmed or corrected.

Numerous newspapers, some long gone, yielded information and illustrations and I am grateful to Archant (Norfolk) Ltd for permission to publish from several different titles.

The staff of the National Archives, Norfolk Heritage Centre, Norfolk Record Office and Archant Press Library guided and kept the research on the right track, and the departments of Norwich City Council responsible for the Guildhall and the Earlham Cemetery gave permission to view and record matters within their purview – and supplied assisting staff. My thanks to all those unnamed persons in those organisations who so willingly and materially helped.

Some can be thanked by name: John Mason for his probing of police history, Philip Yaxley for his in-depth revelations of Wymondham history, Derek James for information and a pipeline to the public, Mike Page for excellent aerial photography, and Richard Barham, Peter Billington, Roger Brighton, Alan Brown, Dave Davies, John Dye, Herbert and Hilda Lines, John McLennan (now deceased), George Piercy (now deceased), Peter Pilgram, Jonathan and George Plunkett, Roger Sandall, Eddie Spelman, Malcolm Watt and Clive and Frieda Wilkins-Jones for their assistance in unearthing details of times past.

Special thanks go to modern illustrators capturing a previously un-pictured past, Terry George and Dave Rowlands, and to all who supplied illustrations or the means to obtain them. Every effort has been made to identify copyright ownership and where pictures are not apparently copy-righted they are source credited. Pictures not apparently copyrighted and from multiple sources are not credited.

I am sensitive to those touched by the tragedies in this book and appreciate their co-operation and understanding. I am especially grateful to Evelyn Cousins for her fortitude and recall of painful times. She expressed a view that talking and writing of a loved one can in a sense bring them to life again. I hope that is the case and this book is so dedicated. History is not always nice but it is informative, educational and within the public domain. I am grateful to all who supported this view.

M. Morson, 2006

Introduction

ll homicide is horrific and tragic. What follows in this book is both representative and selective, identifying the remarkable, gruesome, piteous and poignant, noting milestones in investigations and executions, applying twenty-first century eyes to more primitive times.

The time frame for *Norwich Murders* is the beginning of the Norwich City Police in 1836 to its conclusion in 1968. The geography is, however, necessarily elastic. The city has long had a hinterland with shifting boundaries administered by different authorities, themselves changing with time. It follows that the research for this book sees the city in its widest sense and murders near Norwich, involving both city and county police forces, are included.

Looking at early murders it has to be remembered that the police were untrained and driven more by desire and application than skill. They did not take statements, had no conception of scientific or forensic evidence and could not benefit from fingerprints, blood grouping or photography, while their transport and communications were those of the age, often less so. The status of the police was such that they were commanded by Magistrates and the gentry and not until the latter part of the nineteenth century were they allowed to question prisoners and suspects. They had disciplinary troubles, mainly related to drunkenness, and most of them suffered from a poor education. But they were pioneers. They were men of their time. And they solved murders.

The twentieth century came as an improving age in murder investigation but constant in all murders is the evil in the deliberate taking of another's life, and the sorrow of the innocent. This chronicle looks at Norwich's most memorable cases.

CHAPTER 1

Death of a Policeman
The Murder of Police
Constable William Callow
1848

The poverty and privations of the middle nineteenth century were well exampled in the city of Norwich. The majority of its inhabitants were crammed into squalid and inadequate houses fed by narrow lanes and pocket-sized yards, dependent upon primitive and shared sanitation, dragging water from wells or the fouled river and struggling for sufficient food and warmth. Street disturbances were not uncommon, usually prompted and fuelled by the ready availability and cheapness of ale, but in May and June 1848 riot and murder gripped the city, beginning at that symbol of hard times, the workhouse. Drunkenness was not the root cause for this tumult and tragedy, although it played a part inasmuch as the policeman was allegedly drunk, disorder flowed from the right of a husband to sleep with his wife.

The workhouse at St Andrew's Bridge Street (previously called Blackfriars, eventually part of St George's Street) usually contained over 250 men, women and children, the total and turnover varying with an unremitting death rate. They were bound by hard work and hard rules. The trouble began with a new rule, made by the Poor Law Commissioners under an enabling Act of Parliament, decreeing that husbands should be separated from their wives at night. This edict was roundly condemned by the local movement of Chartists, vigorously led by John Love.

On Tuesday, 23 May, Love had himself and his wife admitted to the workhouse ostensibly to challenge the separation law. At retirement time he 'assumed affection' (as the *Norfolk Chronicle* put it) for his wife and refused to be parted from her. (The *Chronicle* also reported he was 'in the habit of frequently beating' her). Constable Griggs was called to the dispute and, along with a workhouse porter, was 'violently assaulted' by persons rushing in to assist Love. The 'greatest disorder' prevailed, reported the *Norfolk Chronicle*.

Magistrates sentenced Love to one month in prison and in his absence a handbill opposing the separation law was circulated throughout the city. The *Norfolk Chronicle* was unsympathetic. They wrote of 'unthinking or evil disposed men refusing to submit to the law' and of 'a scandalous handbill'.

Further trouble was inevitable and on Friday of that same week eleven men refused to be separated from their wives. Counselling and persuasion by the Master of the Workhouse, William Lowne, failed and they were given in charge to the police to be taken before the Magistrates. The men did not resist.

The Norwich City Police had been born in 1836 with a Superintendent and eighteen men and by 1848 could muster around eighty men, but only with the inclusion of the city Night Watch of thirty-two men (used as policemen but not officially incorporated into the force until 1852). Continually beset with resignations and dismissals, the force had a turnover in some years of as much as fifty per cent. If you were twenty-five to fifty years of age, in good health and at least five feet six inches in height you were eligible to join a force that was untrained, inexperienced and suffered a discipline problem, mainly alcohol driven. The press were generally supportive though one article commented that some of the city police were 'lacking in shrewdness, activity and intelligence'.

The 'refractory paupers', as the press called the eleven, were Jonathan Moore, Benjamin Banham, John Banham, Robert Blackburn, Matthew Beales, Robert Duffield, James Mackley, William Johnson, Jeremiah Francis, John Hook and John Dunn. Appearing

Figures 1.1 & 1.2. Norwich Police Constables. Police Archive

before the Magistrates they received support from an unlikely quarter. The Governor of the Court of Guardians, Mr Beckwith, prosecuting on behalf of the commissioners, said the separation law was not a good law. This statement caused a sensation. The Magistrates, presided over by Mayor George Coleman, asked Beckwith if he wished to withdraw the charges. Beckwith replied that he did not because his job was to administer the law even if he didn't agree with it. He attributed the men's predicament to the 'fault of cowards who had led them into trouble'.

More sensation! Two Magistrates, Mr Palmer and Mr Hudson, said they could not preside over such circumstances and withdrew. The Court adjourned in disarray but later reformed with Palmer and Hudson present.

The Magistrates tried to persuade the defendants to accept the separation law, promising they would be returned to the workhouse without further punishment. The men protested the unfairness of separating a man from his wife at night and some said they were prepared to go to jail while others said they would be transported before being separated from their wives. Johnson said he would only accept the law of the government and was unimpressed when told it was the law of the government.

The Magistrates sentenced the men to twenty-one days' imprisonment. Johnson then asked if the Magistrates could demand they take their wives again and Mr Palmer observed, 'That was the reason then that they wanted to go to prison, to get rid of their wives'. The Court resounded with laughter. Sympathy, counselling and understanding had attended the proceedings, and at the end – humour. But these proceedings were to be the foundations of bitterness, aggression, riot and tragedy. The defiant eleven were taken to the City Gaol at St Giles.

At 9.30 am, Friday, 16 June 1848, the men were released and enthusiastically greeted outside the gaol by 'fifty or sixty persons', a fact that did not escape the attention of the Mayor and police. Trouble was expected, and had been openly spoken of in the city.

The men's wives had remained in the workhouse and had 'conducted themselves with great propriety' while awaiting the return of their husbands but the eleven, and welcoming friends, began a celebratory trawl through public houses before, refreshed and emboldened, they led a procession estimated at 300 strong through the city carrying a banner depicting John Love being beaten by the police. They also carried improvised collecting boxes, which they thrust into people's faces accompanied by a growled demand for a financial contribution. Many met this procession too late to turn away, and later complained.

The progress of the procession, and the behaviour of those forming it, was relayed to eleven wives waiting at the workhouse and three of them proposed setting out to join, or perhaps capture, their husbands. They were advised they would not be allowed back and they consequently stayed.

The police were also monitoring events. They had been assembling since eight o'clock in the morning and before midday a combined force of Constables and Night Watchmen were in a state of readiness. In command was Superintendent Peter Yarington (spelt Yarrington in some documents), assisted by his father, Superintendent William Yarington, commander of the Night Watch. Overall control rested with the Mayor, George Coleman.

The workhouse eleven and their supporters spent the afternoon much as they had the morning while the police assembled at St Andrew's Plain and drilled, and waited, and, like the processional malcontents, drank beer. Superintendent William Yarington noted that eighty officers were in the morning supplied with half a barrel of porter, which, according to him, worked out at two pints per man, and a portion of bread and cheese. In the afternoon they were recalled to the Guildhall Police Station and supplied with a pint of beer and four pennyworth of meat and bread. The Night Watch was on continuous duty for twelve hours and the day Constables for fourteen hours.

At seven o'clock the eleven men made their way to the workhouse and went into the day room with their wives. Their supporters swirled into a jostling noisy crowd on St Andrew's Plain, waiting in menacing expectation, growing in number. Inside the workhouse men and wives had supper together, the standard fare of six ounces of bread, half an ounce of butter and half a pint of tea. They remained together until nine o'clock when William Lowne reminded them they had to go to bed for the night. All eleven refused to retire unless their wives went with them. After an ale-charged day the men had no difficulty telling Lowne what he could do with his separation rule. He reminded them that he had no control over the rules and the workhouse 'did not allow the privacy being afforded to a man and wife so requisite in the hours of retirement'. The men maintained their refusal. The crowd remained noisily evident outside, waiting, and the police remained on stand-by, waiting. The hour of retirement was always going to be boiling point in a day of simmering tension.

William Lowne sent for the Mayor who, by one account, was already in the hall of the workhouse. The Mayor was accompanied by Magistrates, Captain Money and Mr Bolingbroke, and a contingent of thirty police

Figure 1.3. St Andrew's Plain, scene of a riotous assembly. Norfolk County Council Library & Information Service

officers headed by Superintendent Peter Yarington. Ten police officers were stationed in nearby streets.

The arrival of police and Magistrates at the workhouse was greeted with hoots, whistles and jeers by the swelling crowd, now estimated at 2000 in addition to those loitering in streets on the route between the workhouse and the Guildhall Police Station. Women were seen to be gathering stones within their aprons, and men were similarly filling their pockets.

The defiant eleven exuded confidence, clearly expecting the failure of any attempt to arrest and move them into custody. Such confidence, even if inspired by lingering intoxication, was not entirely misplaced. A raucous crowd would surely overwhelm an untrained and inexperienced platoon of policemen inappropriately dressed in leather top hats and swallow tail coats, defensively equipped only with staves. Crowd control and the maintenance of public order were disciplines the early police picked up as they went along. Today's commando-like officer would be protected by padded clothing, shield, visor and long truncheon, and trained to act in a formation, psychologically using noise and counter intimidation to repel an attacking crowd. Spare a thought for these ill-equipped 1848 pioneers, some of whom would not pass a modern day medical to enter the force in the first place.

The Mayor again tried persuasion on the eleven. A report says he 'argued at length'. And he achieved a measure of success. Dunn agreed to go to bed, and went. Blackburn also agreed to go to bed but it is said 'the women exclaimed against him' and he then said, 'Well, then, I'll go to jail.' Hook, apparently not enthusiastic about the impending revolt, agreed to go with his wife to the St Faith's workhouse. The others steadfastly refused to go to bed without their wives and were arrested. They offered no resistance and quietly waited to be escorted from the building.

Police and prisoners appeared before the crowd, shuffling into a pre-arranged box formation, the prisoners in the centre. The crowd greeted Magistrates and police with groans and hooting and the prisoners with cheers. The Mayor intended to press on past the Guildhall Police Station straight to the City Gaol, possibly wary of a siege of the Guildhall. An emissary was sent to the City Gaol to forewarn warders to be ready to fling the gates open because the column would be coming at a fast pace.

The column took off at the quick-step, charging up the plain 'the mob flying in all directions before them but closing up again behind, hooting and yelling and throwing stones'. In this manner the column charged along St Andrew's Broad Street (now St Andrew's) and into Post Office

Figure 1.4. Route of an uprising. Norfolk County Council Library & Information Service

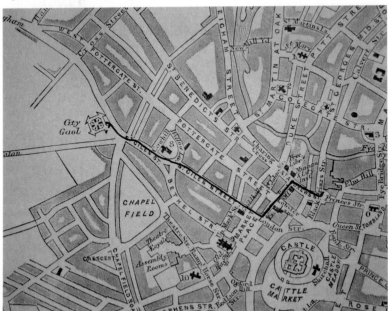

Figures 1.5 & 1.6. Early nineteenth century when trams are running where police and Magistrates once quick-stepped under a hail of missiles. Guildhall Hill (1.5) and St Giles Street (1.6) lead towards St Giles Church, seen in the distance, and the final battle.
Tydeman & Norfolk County Council Library & Information Service

Street (now Exchange Street), into Guildhall Hill, past the police station and into St Giles Street. Volleys of stones fell upon police and prisoners alike, and the yelling was described as 'terrific', an added note being 'particularly from the women'. Policemen's top hats, made of strong leather, were beaten in and numerous backs were scarred; 'as they had been flogged' was one description. Police uniforms were not in any case of the best material, described on one inspection as 'wretched'.

Superintendent Yarington had ordered there should be no looking back and heads must be kept down. In this manner they progressed, the back row of police pushing those in front, which included the prisoners, and at one stage stumbling through impetus and losing contact with those in front. Quickly reforming they pressed on and entered St Giles Street at a run. The prisoners offered no resistance and reportedly begged the crowd to desist because they were being injured by missiles that included bottles and brickbats. (Three prisoners were injured.)

At St Giles Plain, the open space before the gaol, there was more shouting and stone throwing as the gaol gates flew open and police, prisoners, Mayor and Magistrates charged through. The gates slammed shut before the mob, from which a voice cried, 'Goodnight brave fellows.'

A twenty-first century policeman would have been proud of the battered, bruised and bleeding officers who were now breathlessly recovering in the sanctuary of the gaol, their objective realised. William Callow was one of those officers. He was fifty-two years of age, with five children, an agricultural labourer and 'currier' (leather tanner) before he joined the force in January, 1846 at the upper age limit of fifty. For the previous eighteen months Callow had been in poor health following an accident whilst on duty. He was seen in the gaol with blood trickling from his

Figure 1.7. Commotion, riot and death. Terry George

Figure 1.8. St Giles Church in 1896, overlooking where Constable Callow fell. Norfolk County Council Library & Information Service

head, a condition that did not warrant special attention because several officers were marked by cuts.

The crowd outside the gaol did not disperse and there was more stone throwing, some hitting the gates and some raining into the gaol yard. How the police reacted to this continued disturbance is variously described. Some reports have the police charging from the gaol with raised truncheons intent upon clearing the streets, and in some eyes intent upon payback. There was a police charge, and truncheons were raised, and used, but there is evidence that these actions occurred after they had left the gaol and been surrounded. It remains an area of controversy but the statements of Magistrates, police and independent witnesses indicate that the gaol gates were opened to cheers and abuse and the police marched out.

The crowd fell back, the police driving and dividing them into a group retreating into St Giles Street and a splinter group going off into Unthank Road. The Mayor left the gaol several yards behind the police (he admitted he had stayed behind to obtain a glass of beer), just in time to grab stone-thrower William Wood and push him inside the gaol gates.

As one section of the crowd backed away along St Giles Street the Unthank Road splinter group fell in behind the police, throwing stones. Constable Callow, in the back row, flanked by Constables Osborne and Turner, was struck on the head and driven forward, only holding up because of the policemen in the row in front. He was heard to gasp that he had 'got a rum un' on his head.

Superintendent Yarington ordered an about turn and truncheons were drawn, although some observers would say that truncheons had been drawn before then. What is not in dispute is that the police wheeled round and with raised truncheons charged their attackers, leaving behind a dazed Constable Callow with blood pouring from his head. David Girdlestone helped the injured Constable into his shop, the officer gasping, 'For God's sake, open my stock.'

The sequence of the following action is fragmentary. Pockets of disturbance were quelled in the vicinity of the City Gaol, St Giles, Unthank Road, the Guildhall and Gentleman's Walk. There are differing accounts of individual confrontations during this period, depending whether the account giver was supporting or opposing authority, or in some cases keenly watching and in sympathy with one side or the other. Some would later accuse the police of brutality with harrowing tales of truncheons flailing against innocent and respectable 'passers-by', an old man 'cudgelled' to the ground and begging for mercy, a child with blood running from a head wound and a distressed woman with a dented bonnet.

In St Giles Street policemen sought to discover the fate of their colleague and were roundly abused by onlookers, including Isaac Williams who persisted in calling the officers 'cowardly scoundrels', among other things, refusing to go away or shut up until Inspector Robert Thompson silenced him by striking him in the mouth. Williams, recovering from the blow, was then arrested for obstruction by Sergeant Edward Peck.

On Gentleman's Walk a rowdy group confronted Constable Ecclestone and he told them to go away. Henry Bradbury argued his right to remain and a stone was thrown, striking the Constable on the head. The Constable arrested Bradbury.

Near 11 pm a strange confrontation occurred. Fifty or more persons had assembled outside the Guildhall in a state of muted discontent and officers were attempting to move them away from the main door when Mr T Springfield, a Magistrate, arrived and asked what was going on. If he really didn't know then he must have been the only person in Norwich who didn't. Springfield had been Mayor in 1836 when the Norwich City Police had been formed.

Constable William Stamp told Springfield what had been going on, mentioning three injured officers inside the station and producing his top hat that had been stoned through, saying, 'See what they have done.'

Springfield replied, 'Pooh, pooh! That is nothing at all; if they make bad laws you must abide by the consequences.' The listening crowd seemed quite pleased with that statement. Captain Money heard what was said and would give evidence accordingly.

Extra police stayed on duty until midnight by which time the threat of further disorder had diminished. A traumatic day had become history.

Five Constables received injuries removing them from police duties. Constable Barnard had suffered a spinal injury and the others, including Callow and Ecclestone, suffered head wounds. Constable Callow was, according to the *Norfolk Chronicle*, in a 'precarious state' while the *Norwich Mercury* thought 'death is hourly expected'. Wherever the newspapers gleaned their opinions it was not from the Police Surgeon, William Nichols. Callow had been taken home to Union Place where he was treated by the surgeon. Nichols described a cut to the back of the head as 'not very deep' but one sustained above the right eyebrow was through to the bone. Both wounds were bruised and consistent with a blow from an 'angular substance such as a stone'.

The day following the riot, Saturday, 17 June, the Mayor decided to deal expeditiously with all charges arising from the disturbances. His thinking was to remove any festering discontent that might translate into open support for the unconvicted. Following on from this reasoning, and fearing demonstrations at the Guildhall Police Court, the Mayor and Magistrates adjourned to the City Gaol to sit in judgement upon the nine workhouse men nursing headaches from a day of ale and missiles.

The Mayor's fellow Magistrates at the gaol were Mr Bolingbroke and Mr Barnard. It raises the interesting situation of men as witnesses and also sitting in judgement. Furthermore, the Mayor had a meeting with Mr Beckwith to decide who the ringleaders were, proposing that

Figure 1.9. Norwich City Gaol. Alan Brown

those who had been supposedly led could be leniently dealt with. This could be seen as an adjudication awaiting the rubber stamp of a trial.

The identified ringleaders were taken first but Jonathan Moore took exception to the place of trial. He said, 'This is a prison, not a place to hear a case.' He did not deny the offence and spoke of the hardship of being separated from his wife. The Mayor said his case was one of the worst and sentenced him to forty-two days' hard labour.

William Johnson also objected to the trial venue but did not dispute the facts of the case. He said the separation rule was illegal and it was a hardship to separate a man from his wife just because he was poor. He was sentenced to twenty-eight days' hard labour.

Robert Duffield, a shoemaker with five children, admitted the facts and said he only wanted a little relief for himself so that he could go out and find work and take his family out of the workhouse. Mr Lowne, the Master, told the Court that he had got Duffield work but the man had refused to go claiming that he did not have any tools. The Magistrates sentenced Duffield to twenty-eight days' hard labour.

The fourth identified ringleader, John Banham, a man with one child, said he did not wish to be in the workhouse or in jail and he was every week in expectation of work. Lowne told the Magistrates that Banham behaved very badly in the workhouse. They sentenced him to twenty-one days' hard labour.

The remaining men, Benjamin Banham, James Mackley (another with five children), Robert Blackburn, Matthew Beales and Jeremiah Francis, were each in turn brought in and asked if they were willing to go back to the workhouse and obey the rules, in such case they would be discharged from the Court. The men asked if they would be allowed to leave the workhouse to seek work and they were told that if there was a reasonable chance of them securing work the House Committee would consider their request. They all agreed and were discharged.

The Mayor and Magistrates returned to the Guildhall to deal with the other cases – three in all. Here they were joined by other Magistrates, including Captain Money and Mr Hudson. The first case charged William Wood of Union Place, detained by the Mayor, with throwing a stone at the City Gaol. The Mayor and Captain Money gave evidence that Wood had thrown a stone and Wood denied it. He explained that he had been smoking a pipe and had thrown it as an act of frustration not intending to hit or hurt anybody, which he hadn't. He was fined £2 or fourteen days' imprisonment in default.

Henry Bradbury of St Gregory's was charged with assaulting Constable Ecclestone and the Constable showed the Court where he had been struck on the head by a stone. Bradbury said somebody else had thrown the stone. The Magistrates fined him £5 with one month's imprisonment in default.

The third case was a revelation of nineteenth century attitudes. Isaac Williams from Heigham, a respectable man with an unblemished reputation, and acquainted with Superintendent Peter Yarington, appeared charged with obstructing Inspector Thompson, probably still feeling the weight of the blow he had received from that officer. He admitted calling the police 'cowardly scoundrels' (some versions of this episode record 'cowardly rascals') and explained that he was incensed at seeing 'respectable young men knocked about'. He said he had gone to St Giles after being informed that an old gentleman had been injured and he had no interest in promoting a disturbance or obstructing the police. Magistrate Mr Hudson commented that stopping and insulting the police was not the way to preserve the peace.

Williams complained that Inspector Thompson had struck him in the mouth, not denied by the officer, and this brought cries of 'shame, shame' from the public gallery, swiftly silenced by Superintendent Yarington.

Mr Hudson said that if Williams used the language attributed to him 'the policeman served him perfectly right'. He (Mr Hudson) did not see why policemen should be insulted in that way. Williams must now have guessed which way his case was going.

Sergeant Peck said that Inspector Thompson's 'temper was up' and Williams was arrested because he was exciting the crowd – not to mention Inspector Thompson. (Inspector Robert Thompson's career was to be punctuated by disciplinary proceedings for drunkenness and he was eventually dismissed.)

Superintendent Peter Yarington gave evidence in support of Isaac Williams's character and reputation and said he had previously helped the police. The courtroom was cleared while the Magistrates consulted. Their decision was that Williams was 'Guilty' and he was fined £3 or three weeks' imprisonment in default. Williams paid the fine, a sadder and wiser man and no longer enamoured with the Norwich City Police.

On the Monday following the Court cases the condition of Constable Callow worsened. The deep wound on his forehead had become infected. His general poor health became a barrier to fighting the infection and the police surgeon expressed some concern.

Others expressed concern over police tactics and the *Norfolk News* thought the police had been too aggressive, saying it had names of persons witnessing or the victim of police assaults. The newspaper suggested the police were drunk and the Magistrates biased and 'infected with mob-phobia due to the state of Europe'. It produced an article accusing the police of 'bludgeoning indiscriminately the nearest, the weakest and the worst runners', and while regretting that an attempt had been made to 'interrupt' the police on their way to the gaol claimed only one stone had been thrown.

The *Norfolk News* called for an inquiry into the Norwich City Police and their handling of the riot and sent letters it had received to the Home Secretary. The published letter of Thomas Jarrold is repeated below.

I beg most respectfully to request that you will cause enquiry to be made into the conduct of the police force in the violent attack upon a crowd of persons on Friday evening the 16th. I passed through the assembly on my return from a walk in the country (after business) about three minutes before the police made their violent charge and I beg to add all were quiet, and most appeared to have collected by curiosity, and were quietly talking to one another. I have not the least sympathy with the men who had been committed for workhouse insubordination but I have the firmest conviction that the violent attack on a crowd of persons, for the most part well-conducted and respectable, *without giving the least warning,* [letter writer's italics] was imprudent and unwarrantable, both on the part of the police and the Magistrates who directed it. Before calling out the military it is imperative to read the riot act. A policeman's staff may give just as deadly a blow to a respectable person as a dragoon's sword. I am quite sure the matter cannot rest where it is; I therefore trust you will, for the satisfaction of a peaceable population, instruct that a strict enquiry be made into the matter.

C J Bunting wrote on similar lines, saying, 'I am desirous of acquainting you with the fact that the feeling of enmity now existing towards the police on the part of a large portion of my fellow citizens is such as to endanger public safety.' He criticised police actions and called for a 'minute investigation of the whole proceedings'.

The Home Secretary, Sir George Grey, wrote to the Mayor, George Coleman, requiring a report. The Mayor's report was an unrepentant account. He stated that it had been necessary to clear the streets and, referring to the disturbance, said, 'Had it not been put down at once it would have led to a serious outbreak.' He said it had been an honour to be in charge and in the same circumstances he would do exactly the same again. He finished by pointing out that Thomas Jarrold was the proprietor of the *Norfolk News*, which he described as a 'Chartist newspaper', and Bunting was one of his employees.

The Home Secretary wrote back to say that the Mayor's report was 'quite satisfactory'. But it was not over. Allegations against the police were to receive another public airing.

Constable William Callow died at his home on the Friday afternoon, one week after the riot that led to his death. That same afternoon the Coroner, Mr Wilde, convened an inquest at the *Goldbeater's Arms* in Bethel Street and empanelled a 'very respectable jury'. After the jury had viewed the body Inspector Minns gave evidence of identity and proceedings were formally adjourned to await a post mortem.

The inquest re-convened on Monday, 26 June, in the Council Chamber of the Guildhall. Police Surgeon Nichols described the wounds on Callow's head and said the deepest one had become infected with a 'peculiar inflammation'. He said he had conducted a post-mortem examination which confirmed his diagnosis. He said that Callow was 'not a robust man', 'ailing for nearly a year and a half', but it was his opinion that he would still be alive if he had not received the blows to the head.

A modern observer may question what a middle-aged, ailing and less than robust man was doing in the police force but it must be remembered that these were pioneering days when standards in the police were markedly different to later years. Men needed work and would profess themselves to a fitness and capability to obtain and maintain it. William Callow was as much a victim of his time as he was of a rioter's stone.

The Coroner sought to obtain evidence of the disturbances leading to Callow's injuries. This turned into as much a defence of police action as an examination into the assault upon Constable Callow.

The Mayor, in answer to a juror, said, 'The conduct of the police was firm and determined, and they merely did their duty.'

Another juror asked if was necessary for the police to use their truncheons and the Town Clerk, Mr Staff, representing the Callow family, said the police had been ordered to produce truncheons. The Mayor said they had been showered with stones on the way to the gaol and after delivering the prisoners he had ordered the streets to be cleared, and the police had carried out that order with firmness. The Mayor said that he had seen Callow with blood running down his face.

Captain Money, called to the witness box, corroborated the Mayor's evidence and said the police had not been intoxicated and he had not seen men behave better in his life.

Constables Thomas Osborne and Edward Turner gave evidence of Callow being hit by a stone and David Girdlestone gave evidence of assisting the injured Constable.

Sergeant Peck said that after leaving the gaol the stones 'became so killing' they were ordered to 'right about face' following which they drove the crowd before them. He heard the Mayor give the order not to injure women and children and he saw no women or children injured. If such persons were knocked over it was by the running crowd. He said he saw a great many women and children and he advised them to go away. In answer to the Coroner Sergeant Peck said that up to the time the police were ordered to about face he saw no blows struck, and he never saw men keep their temper so well under provocation.

The inquiry into the death of Constable Callow became integral with an investigation into police behaviour and to this end John Druery became an esteemed witness. Druery was a barrister-at-law and had been delayed by the crowd. He said he saw the police column leaving the gaol and marching down St Giles Street, and being stoned from the rear. The Coroner referred to him as 'a gentleman who understands these matters, and quite competent to give an opinion', and then asked his opinion of the conduct of the police.

Druery replied, 'I have no doubt that their conduct was as orderly as could be desired. I was repeatedly passed by the police, and seen by them, but not disturbed. I think their conduct was so forbearing that they received showers of stones before they turned on the mob.'

The Coroner asked if the police had behaved 'rashly' and Druery replied, 'Certainly not.' He added that he thought the crowd was an illegal assembly and if they had not been dispersed some of the police would have been killed. (One was!)

The hearing concluded that day with the Coroner and the Town Clerk calling for persons expressing opinions that the police behaved improperly to come forward, failing which accusations and charges made against the police 'went for nothing'.

The inquest resumed on Tuesday, 27 June, and looked into allegations that the police had been intoxicated. Superintendent William Yarington, head of the Night Watch, gave evidence of his men's deployment and refreshment. The sum of his evidence was that no man should have had more than three pints of beer or porter during the course of twelve hours of duty. His son, Superintendent Peter Yarington gave similar evidence as it related to the day police. Their evidence was not contentious, again a sign of the times.

Digressing from the main purpose of the inquest the foreman of the jury asked for a statement they had heard, concerning the conduct of one of the Magistrates, to be confirmed. He was alluding to Mr Springfield's appearance at the Guildhall and his remarks to Constable Stamp. The Coroner accordingly sent for Constable Stamp and he gave evidence that Springfield thought the police injuries were 'nothing at all' and they should abide by the consequences of bad laws. The Coroner asked the jury if they wanted Mr Springfield to give evidence and the foreman said they did. The inquest was adjourned in order that he could be found.

Mr Springfield could not be found and the inquest continued. The Coroner directed the jury, saying that the verdict appeared to him to be 'one of murder against some person or persons unknown'.

The jury duly returned a verdict of 'wilful murder', the foreman adding that they did not wish to stop at the verdict. They desired from the evidence laid before them to record their approbation of the conduct of the police, believing they acted with the greatest forbearance, and they 'begged to suggest' that a memorial be presented to the Secretary of State on behalf of the widow and five children of the late William Callow.

The Coroner thanked them and said he concurred with every word. He said that to his great surprise the evidence had come out exactly the opposite to what he had supposed, for he had come into the room with the impression the police had behaved rashly. He said he would undertake to present their recommendation in respect of the widow to the proper quarter.

The killer, or killers, of William Callow were never found, perhaps not surprising in the circumstances. Did the thrower of the fatal stone know upon whom it landed? Or even care?

Mrs Callow received two payments of £1 from the Watch Committee, described in minutes as 'temporary relief', and a Sub-Committee was set up to consider a subscription, the result of which is not recorded.

The Watch Committee also wrote to solicitors and the press to elicit names of persons keen to charge the police with drunkenness and assault. The replies claimed privilege and pointed out that the Coroner had publicly made the same request and persons could individually come forward if they so wished. Nobody came forward.

William Callow was the victim of a revolt the cause of which he probably sympathised with. The rebels certainly had no dispute with him, other than he had been drawn against their cause in the course of his duty. Callow was a middle-aged man seeking work within an infant police force, destined to go into history as the only Norwich police officer ever to be murdered. The tragic irony is that the family he sought to provide for became destitute through something inspired by the poor in the city.

CHAPTER 2

Death of a Judge
The Murders of the Norwich
Recorder and his son
1848

t is almost an impertinence to write of the murders in 1848 of the Norwich Recorder and his son for no case has secured so much public interest and spawned so many written accounts and was, and still is, so fascinating yet substantially devoid of contention. Only the murderer disputed the evidence.

The notoriety of the case and the wealth of books, novels, narratives, exhibitions, models, plays and films means there is inevitably some blurring of issues. The account that follows seeks to dispel any mistiness and reveal new depths; anyway, no chronicle of Norwich murders can possibly omit this case.

The lasting public interest may be explained by the eminence of the victim, Isaac Jermy (Preston), Recorder of Norwich Quarter Sessions, and the audacity and ruthlessness of his murderer, James Blomfield Rush, a man with property and servants. Rush had planned the killing in great detail, though possibly not the escalating confrontation that eventually took place.

The scene of the crime, and the crux and inspiration for incidents and ill-will that had gone before, was Stanfield Hall, an Elizabethan moated mansion standing in open countryside two and a half miles from the small market town of Wymondham and nine miles from Norwich. The house, grounds and attendant farms, were part of the estate of the Jermy family but the line ran out with William Jermy, or would have done except that in 1752 he married his solicitor's sister, Frances Preston. He died a few weeks later.

William Jermy's will stipulated that his wife should inherit the estate followed by *named* Prestons and their heirs, failing which the nearest related male Jermy. Inheritors, however, were required to have or take the name Jermy.

Frances Jermy nee Preston died in 1791, creating a problem. She had survived all the Prestons named in William Jermy's will. The Reverend George Preston's entitlement to the estate may therefore have been dubious, but it was not until his death in 1837 that trouble flared. He had willed Stanfield Hall, its land and farms, to his eldest son, Isaac, barrister-at-law and Recorder of Norwich. The Reverend had not taken the Jermy name but Isaac had named his eldest son, Isaac Jermy Preston, this to later lead to an interesting duplication.

Isaac, the Recorder, distrusted his father's bailiff, a man whom the Reverend had treated kindly. James Blomfield Rush (Bloomfield and Blomefield appear in

Figure 2.1. Isaac Jermy. Group Archive Aviva Plc

various reports and documents) tenant farmer at Felmingham, lived at Stanfield Hall Farm and owned Potash Farm. A short thick-set man of hunched appearance and indifferent temperament, he had a chequered past. He was born in 1800, the illegitimate son of Mary Blomfield (she successfully sued the father for breach of promise) and acquired his surname when Mary married John Rush, a farmer. He grew up with a grammar school education and in 1824 became a tenant farmer at Aylsham. He married Susannah Soames in that same year and they had ten children, one dying in infancy.

Rush moved to a farm at Wood Dalling where he was accused of arson, but not convicted, and in another incident charged with aiding and abetting workers involved in 'machine breaking'. He was bound over to keep the peace. He moved to Felmingham and worked as an auctioneer while renting a farm from the Reverend George Preston. His step-father rented the neighbouring farm.

Isaac Preston, the Recorder, newly in ownership of Stanfield Hall but not in residence, advertised an auction to be held at the hall of furniture and effects, to take place on 26 and 27 June 1838. On the second day of the auction a man named John Larner arrived and claimed the house and estate. He said he was the heir through the Jermy family, disconcerting Isaac Preston with his knowledge of the provisions of William Jermy's

Figure 2.2. Stanfield Hall.

will. Larner knew of the required continuance of the Jermy name, also a stipulation that the Stanfield Hall library should not be sold, which was exactly what Isaac Preston was doing.

Larner had travelled from London with a man named Daniel Wingfield, variously described as Larner's 'adviser' or 'attorney', in reality an 'oil and colour man' (shopkeeper who sold oil). It is suspected that Larner learned of the auction from Rush.

John Larner purported to be the cousin of Thomas Jermy – an elderly and illiterate London man, the illiteracy to assume great importance at a later date, supposedly related to a John Jermy of Great Yarmouth.

Isaac Preston had Larner and Wingfield escorted off the premises and stopped the auction. His next action reflected the serious view he took of the intrusion. He petitioned the Queen to grant a warrant to change the Preston surname to Jermy. It says something of his importance that the warrant was promptly granted, resulting in his son becoming Isaac Jermy Jermy.

Figure 2.3. James Blomfield Rush. Teignmouth Shore Collection

Isaac Preston, (to become Jermy), was born in 1789 and educated at Oxford University. He married Mary Beevor, who came from a noble family, and they had a son Isaac, (soon to be a double Jermy) and a daughter. Mary died in 1823 and he remarried in 1832 to Fanny Jephson. She gave him another daughter, Isabella. Fanny died in 1835. Isaac Preston enjoyed power and influence in the forelock-tugging days of the first half of the nineteenth century and a well dressed appearance and haughty demeanour is an unnecessary description. It went with the territory. His next move after Larner's visit was to sell Stanfield Hall to James Blomfield Rush for a fraction of its worth. There is no doubt that Rush was more a conspirator than a beneficiary, even though Isaac Preston didn't trust him. A case of when the devil drives . . .

In August 1838 Rush advertised the Hall for rent and the sale of glasshouses and other materials (Preston selling by proxy?). John Larner responded by distributing handbills stating his right to the estate and on 11 September he arrived at Stanfield Hall with eight 'friends and relatives', occupying the Hall for three to four hours before being expelled by Rush and helpers, Rush probably quietly expressing sympathy for Larner's cause and looking for any advantage that might accrue for himself. Such an association was later admitted by Rush.

The day following his expulsion Larner procured a man to symbolically chop down a tree on the estate. A Parish Constable was called to charge the man before a Magistrate. (The county of Norfolk did not have a professional police force until 1839.) Larner paid the tree feller's fine and issued more handbills. On 20 September he and friends attempted another occupation of the Hall. They were outnumbered and repelled, obviously expected.

On 24 September Larner returned with a force reported to be sixty or seventy strong, a mixture of labourers, tradesman and friends and relatives. Many were named Pearce, many were local. All the men wore laurel leaves in their hats – a kind of identifying uniform. The motive of these men for helping Larner is not known. Perhaps they saw a class struggle.

The tenants of Stanfield Hall barred doors and windows but Larner forced a door and the men swept inside, ejecting tenants and furniture into heavy rain. They then barricaded windows and armed themselves with clubs, rejecting pleas from arriving Parish Constables and Magistrates. Violence broke out when Constable Hubbard captured one of the intruders and was 'bludgeoned to the ground' by the man's rescuing friends.

Constables Pont and Tipple were also assaulted, as was Isaac Jermy when he arrived and read the Riot Act, a reading that left the occupiers unmoved.

It took a detachment of Dragoon Guards to get them out, and then only after the soldiers had loaded ball cartridges and levelled their muskets, the Captain in charge calling for the occupiers to surrender. Reports say sixty-three of the intruders were roped together and taken away in wagons to Norwich Castle, but there is a police record that says the jailer received eighty-three prisoners, packing them six to a cell. Twenty-six of those detained were committed to the Assize on charges of riot and tumult.

The Assize hearing offered a reduction of the charge to simple riot if the accused men would give an undertaking not to approach Stanfield Hall again. This smacks of the influence of Recorder Isaac Jermy and he did speak to that effect in Court; an early example of plea bargaining.

Larner and Wingfield gave undertakings as required and were each sentenced to three months' imprisonment, with the threat of trans-portation in the event of any repeat action against Stanfield Hall. Not fancying a one-way sea voyage they gave up overt action but, as will be seen, not covert activities. To this end Rush became an accomplice, if he wasn't before.

In 1839 a Norwich woman named Dank successfully sued Rush for seduction and breach of promise, adding to his financial worries.

In 1840 Isaac Jermy repurchased Stanfield Hall from James Rush, a previously agreed paper exercise, and moved in with his family and servants.

In October 1844 Rush's step-father was found dead in the kitchen of his home, a discharged gun lying nearby. The inquest delivered a verdict of accidental death.

In November 1844, Susannah Rush died aged forty-six years, leaving James with the responsibility for nine children, aged three to fifteen years. He advertised in *The Times* for a governess and appointed Emily Sandford. She was twenty-six years of age, well educated, the daughter of a well-to-do London family, described as slightly built, pretty and lady-like. She lived variously at Felmingham Farm and Potash Farm and was known locally as 'the widow Mrs James'.

Rush promised marriage to Emily Sandford and she bore him a child, which died in infancy. Emily's mother wrote to her, and she to her mother but it transpired that this correspondence never reached the intended destinations and there can be no doubt that James Rush intercepted the incoming and destroyed the outgoing. He told Emily's mother that her daughter had gone to France.

Rush's mother had been living with him and on 13 August 1848 she died suddenly and mysteriously, aged sixty-eight years. Her will provided for Rush's children on them reaching the age of eighteen years but Rush, now in financial difficulty, forged a codicil that allowed him access. Isaac Jermy had expelled him from Stanfield Hall Farm for non-payment of rent and was pressing for payments on the mortgage Rush had taken out on Potash Farm. That mortgage agreement expired on 30 November 1848, a tragically significant date. When Isaac Jermy brought actions against Rush for breach of covenant and sued for monies owed Rush plunged into bankruptcy. He devised counter measures.

In October 1848 John Larner and Thomas Jermy travelled to Norfolk by arrangement with Rush, expecting to discuss their possession of Felmingham Farm (part of the Jermy estate). Rush failed to appear and they returned to London. Rush then travelled to London with Emily Sandford and met John Larner, Thomas Jermy and a man named Richard Read. Rush produced a written agreement that gave title to Felmingham Farm and properties at Skeyton and North Walsham (part of his mother's estate) to Thomas Jermy as soon as Rush 'could conveniently' put him in possession. The document provided for onward renting to Rush on favourable terms and allowed him to be reimbursed with 'reasonable expenses' occasioned in securing title and possession. The document was agreed, Larner and Jermy making their mark, Emily Sandford and Richard Read signing as witnesses.

Returning to Norfolk Emily was required to append her signature to more documents produced by Rush. These purported to show Isaac Jermy varying and extending the mortgage agreement, and in another cancelling it. She duly signed; still hoping that Rush would seal their union with marriage, as he had originally offered. The fact that James Blomfield Rush did not marry Emily Sandford was one of his biggest mistakes. A wife cannot give evidence against her husband.

In the wet and misty gloom of the evening of 28 November 1848 Stanfield Hall showed as a black shape faintly speckled by interior lights. The occupants were in a leisurely after-dinner state, Isaac Jermy Jermy and his wife Sophia in the drawing room, the Recorder, Isaac Jermy, sitting in the dining room alone, and servants mainly located in the servants' hall. Isabella Preston, the Recorder's daughter, was also in the house, inconspicuous and to remain so. A cloaked figure lurked outside the front porch.

A little after eight o'clock Isaac Jermy left the dining room and made his way to the porch, a regular occurrence at this time. As he appeared in the porch the cloaked figure stepped forward, producing a large pistol and firing into Jermy's chest at such close range his clothing was scorched. Death was instantaneous, Jermy's heart destroyed by a barrage of slugs. The gunman stepped into the mansion, moving quickly, dropping two papers as he hurried along the passage, passing the butler, James Watson, in the act of opening the pantry door.

The Recorder's son, startled by the gunshot, opened the door to the lobby and came upon the cloaked intruder, witnessed by the butler. The intruder fired and Isaac Jermy Jermy fell back. The butler retreated into his pantry.

Eliza Chestney, a housemaid, heard the gunshots from the servants' hall and went to the lobby to investigate, meeting Mrs Jermy Jermy on the way. As they entered the lobby the intruder shot them both, Chestney collapsing to the floor and Mrs Jermy Jermy staggering into a passage. The butler emerged from the pantry and dragged Chestney to the back staircase.

Margaret Read, a cook, had been in the servants' hall with Chestney when the first and second shots rang out, but had not gone to investigate, not until she heard the third and fourth shots. She saw Mrs Jermy Jermy running screaming down the passage followed by a man walking quickly and holding a 'long pistol or short gun'. She described the man as dressed in a cloak or long coat with a small cape, of short and stout build with a very short neck, carrying his head to one side in the manner of James Rush. The instant she saw him she thought she was looking at Rush, even though she did not have a clear view of his face. Chestney was to offer the same opinion, saying the man had 'wide shoulders' and looked like 'Mr Rush'. The butler, Watson, was of the same view, though he thought the face was masked.

The other person to see the gunman was Maria Blanchflower, nurse to Mrs Jermy Jermy. After hearing gunshots and screams she ran to the servants' hall and in the passage saw a man coming towards her. Her brief description was that he was a short, stout man darkly dressed. Such paucity of detail is excusable because on seeing him she turned and fled.

Others did not see but heard. Three young men were standing by the bridge over the moat, talking with two maidservants from the Hall; they all heard a gunshot and one of the men saw a muzzle flash from the Hall. They ran to the lodge gate (away from the Hall) and heard further shots as they ran. They saw nobody.

Stanfield Hall in the aftermath of the shootings became a scene of panic. Outside doors were secured and the alarm bell rung. Two men were obviously dead, two women were seriously injured, others terrified. And the two papers dropped by the intruder cannot have helped.

The papers were notes written in a scrawled, apparently disguised hand, the content as follows:

> There are 7 of us here three of us outside and four of us inside the hall. All armed, as you see us two, if any of you servants offer to leave the Premises or to follow us, you will be shot Dead, therefore all of you keepe in the servants Hall and you will not take any harme; for we only come to take Possession of the Stanfield Property.
>
> Thos Jermy
>
> the Owner.

Also lying in the lobby was the ramrod of a gun, later to be attributed to a blunderbuss.

The outside world was soon to know of the awful events at Stanfield Hall. The groom had heard the commotion from the stables and he waded across the moat, running to Stanfield Hall Farm, there obtaining a horse and riding furiously to Wymondham crying out the alarm to persons he passed on the way. He went to the house of Magistrate William Cann and a moment of history followed. Cann used the new electric telegraph to contact Norwich Magistrates, following which Superintendent Peter Yarington of the Norwich City Police sent a telegraph message to all points along the railway to London. A Norwich Magistrate ordered an armed contingent of Norwich City Police to Wymondham.

Three Inspectors and four Constables went in post chaises to Stanfield Hall and were joined by Constable Pont of the Rural Force. They viewed a scene of carnage and confusion.

Figure 2.4. Scene of death, blood on the floor and wall. The lobby at Stanfield Hall, a drawing from the time.

Neighbouring farmers, excited locals from different stations in life, and Magistrates and other notaries had arrived, carriages herding together outside the Hall. Superintendent Yarington travelled to Wymondham by mail train.

The family doctor (also the police surgeon), William Nichols, was summoned from Norwich, later to be joined by surgeon Robert Tunaley from Wymondham. Before the night was out a procession of the necessary, important, comforting and curious had been at Stanfield Hall. The reporter of the *Norfolk Chronicle* described a pool of blood in the lobby from which a trail led to the dining room where the bodies had been laid out. He called it 'a ghastly spectacle'. His report says he was invited to view the bodies.

According to the press the news reached Norwich at eleven o'clock and 'the whole city was in a ferment'. Within the city, and amongst the chattering excitement at Stanfield Hall, the name of one suspect was paramount: it was agreed that James Rush must have committed the murders.

William Cann sent the Norwich officers and Constable Pont to surround Potash Farm. From two o'clock in the morning the officers watched and waited, huddled against damp and cold, peering intently through the November darkness. They may have considered storming Potash Farm with the element of surprise but it didn't happen that way. It was all very civil and English. At a quarter to six they saw a light and Rush's servant, a lad named Solomon Savory, moving around. The police called to him and he roused Rush who unbarred the door. The police piled through the door and Constable John Morter of the city force grabbed Rush and declared, 'You are my prisoner.'

Rush replied, 'Your prisoner! What have I done?'

Constable Pont handcuffed Rush and informed him, 'The two Mr Jermys have been shot and you are suspected of doing it.'

Rush replied, 'Good God! I hope you don't suspect me of doing it.' (He had just been told that they did suspect him.)

Rush asked Morter, 'What time did the affair take place?'

Morter did not answer and Rush, after a pause, said, 'I understand it was done a little after eight o'clock.'

Morter asked, 'From whom, sir, did you understand that?' (He was later to be rebuked by the Coroner for questioning the suspect: a High Court Judge had ruled that it was illegal for policemen to question prisoners or suspects. Anyway, Rush denied he said it.)

Rush said, 'I should have been there last night about that time, had I understood that young Mr Jermy was at home. The young man is a great enemy of mine, but the old gentleman and me have been better friends than we were.'

Rush was placed in the charge of Constable Osborne of the city police while other officers searched the building. Emily Sandford had been roused from her room and she began making tea in the kitchen. Rush told her he had been accused of murdering Mr Jermy and his son and said, 'But you and Savory can clear me, as Savory washed my boots at half-past five, and you know I did not go . . .' he stopped, paused, and said, 'Did they ask you any questions?'

She replied, 'They asked me if you went out in the evening.'

Rush said, 'They had no right to ask such questions. What did you tell them?'

She answered, 'I said you were out between eight and nine for quarter of an hour.'

Rush said, 'I was not out ten minutes.'

Figure 2.5. Landscape of a murder from the Norfolk Chronicle: *extraordinary edition. Stanfield Hall is centre far left and Potash Farm centre far right.* Archant

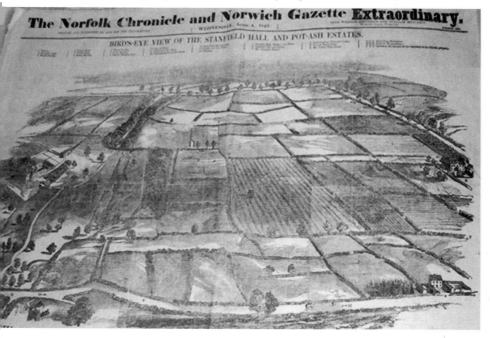

Figure 2.6. Potash Farm, watched by police throughout the night.

The search of the house discovered several pairs of boots, including a damp pair in the bedroom.

In the same bedroom Inspector Robert Thompson of the city police found two loaded fowling pieces with powder flasks and a number of bullets, and a dark cloak that was damp. (The guns, while causing intense interest, were not going to be revealed as the murder weapons. The cloak became an exhibit but was never positively identified by any witness.)

The bedroom also contained a dark curly wig but that was not found until the Friday when Superintendent Hubbersty of the Rural Force looked inside a box in a closet. (Again, the wig became an exhibit and was not positively identified by any witness.)

The original searching officers also missed a loose floorboard, not discovered until the Saturday when Superintendent Witherspoon of the Rural Force prised it up and found the documents forged by Rush in respect of the mortgage, and the agreement made in London between Rush, Larner and Thomas Jermy, all signed by Emily Sandford. Witherspoon assuredly knew where to look after Rush had confided the information to John Cann, solicitor and son of the Magistrate. Rush later said with some bitterness that he thought John Cann was defending him. John Cann was also Clerk to the Justices and had, according to some reports, previously advised John Larner on his claim to Stanfield Hall. John and William Cann were never far from this case.

Rush was taken by pony and gig to the Wymondham Bridewell and that same afternoon to Stanfield Hall where he was examined by Magistrates and identified as the gunman by Mrs Jermy Jermy. He was returned to the Bridewell and retained in custody despite protests and a demeanour, genuine or contrived, that indicated a belief he would shortly be released. (Sir Thomas Beevor, relative of Isaac Jermy's first wife was an examining Magistrate.)

Surgeon William Nichols conducted post-mortems on the bodies, assisted by Robert Tunaley. Both victims had died instantly, the Recorder through slugs fired at close range into the heart, his son, similarly at close range, through slugs penetrating a lung and travelling through the base of the heart and destroying part of the vertebrae. Medical opinion ruled out the fowling pieces found in Potash Farm. The damage to the bodies was such that a blunderbuss seemed the likely weapon.

The bodies remained at Stanford Hall until the funeral on Tuesday, 5 December. Straw was laid outside the Hall to muffle carriage wheels and horses' hooves, hoping not to disturb the injured ladies in the Hall, and curious and commiserating spectators lined the road to Wymondham. When the solemnly plodding procession reached the town they found shops closed and an 'immense concourse' waiting to pay their respects. Wymondham Abbey was filled and ringed with mourners. After the service father and son were laid together in a specially constructed vault at the church, several mourners entering to say their last farewells before it was closed. The *Norfolk Chronicle* reported that at this point the 'midday sun rose in fullest splendour'.

The weeks following the murders saw the conflict and confusion of nineteenth century processes of investigation and administration. On 30 November the Coroner, Edward Press, empanelled a jury at *The King's Head* public house in Wymondham and took them to Stanfield Hall to view the bodies. The inquest then met on four further occasions, taking formal evidence under oath (excepting Solomon Savory who said he didn't understand the oath) and cross examining witnesses.

Over the same period of time the Magistrates continued their examination, meeting on six more occasions after their first visit to Stanfield Hall. Rush cross examined witnesses with bitterness, expressing despair and outrage that he should be suspected, maintaining his innocence, contesting the evidence, arguing with Magistrates and shouting his case as he was threatened with removal.

A farcical situation arose where witnesses were bandied back and forth between two sets of legal proceedings, in some cases the Coroner sending a Constable to retrieve a witness from the Magistrates. Emily Sandford had been taken into custody at the Bridewell, a fact that irked the Coroner's jury wanting to question her. The Magistrates declined to release her so the Coroner moved the inquest from *The King's Head* to the Bridewell for the one witness. Rush became extremely truculent when Sandford gave her evidence.

On 2 December the Magistrates committed Rush to Norwich Castle and held a private hearing there the next day. This turned out to be less than private as persons came and went as they liked, and the press lay in wait and re-interviewed witnesses as they left. The Magistrates examined witnesses again at the castle on 13 and 14 December and on this latter day charged and committed Rush to the Assize for trial. But they had been too hasty. On 19 December they had to produce Rush at Stanfield Hall by writ of *habeas corpus* to hear the evidence of the seriously injured Eliza Chestney.

On 19 December the inquest returned a verdict of murder against Rush, a presumptuous determination but in line with the procedure of the time. More modern times would see a coroner take evidence of identification and cause of death, and then formally adjourn proceedings to await the result of the criminal investigation. And a twentieth century innovation would see committal proceedings undertaken through statements recorded by the police.

While the examinations were taking place the Chief Constable of the Rural Force, Colonel Oakes, reported to his police authority of Magistrates 'circumstances of daring atrocity and premeditation against which not vigilance of your police could have guarded'.

Of the ongoing search for a blunderbuss, he reported, 'Twenty pits have been pumped out and every particle of mud removed from them, that had a pencil case been at the bottom it must inevitably have been found. Fences and ditches have been cut down, and every rabbit or rat hole has been probed to the bottom. Furze and other bushes grubbed up, muck heaps, turnip heaps, mangle worzel heaps removed, turnip fields most minutely examined, plough fields perforated with heavy crowbars, grass fields pierced with iron spears. Every tree in the park has been mounted and minutely examined.' He went on in similar vein about how Potash Farm grounds had been dug up and the building examined by carpenters and tile masons. He finished by saying, 'Such a search was never mounted before.' Some statements come back to haunt the maker. This was one.

In the meantime Constable Morter received a £3 gratuity from the Norwich Watch Committee for making the arrest.

The trial of James Blomfield Rush took place at Norwich before Mr Baron Rolfe, beginning on Thursday, 29 March 1849. Admission was by ticket and the courtroom was crammed 'in every part by gentlemen and ladies of the highest respectability, including several noblemen'. Class ruled.

The prisoner in the dock was dressed in black, confident looking and armed with a sheaf of papers, which he asked time to arrange before the jury was sworn. His hand trembled as he sorted. Finally, he said, 'I am quite ready, my lord.' He was going to defend himself. Another mistake!

The trial lasted until Friday 6 April. The prosecution called witnesses to give evidence of the antipathy between Isaac Jermy and the prisoner, threats by the prisoner, the imminent foreclosure upon Potash Farm, the written agreements between Rush, Larner and Thomas Jermy, and the forged documents found under the floor board at Potash Farm.

Witnesses spoke of Rush making enquiries on 28 November as to whether Isaac Jermy was at home. (A Mrs Bailey would have given evidence that she had seen him near Stanfield Hall on that day, but after questioning by Magistrates, and absorbing the full horror of the events, she had become 'deranged' and been committed to Thorpe Asylum. In those days there was little understanding of trauma occasioned by shock.)

A young boy employed by Rush told the Court that on the day of the murders, on the instructions of Rush, he had laid straw on a direct route from Potash Farm to Stanfield Hall. Constable Futter of the Norwich City Police said the distance of the straw path was seven furlongs.

James Watson, butler, and Margaret Read, cook, confirmed their impression of Rush as the gunman.

Watson declared from the witness box, 'I believe that man was the prisoner.'

Rush blurted out, 'That's not a fair way of putting it.'

The Judge responded, 'I think it was very properly put.'

Rush said that Watson and Read had been 'tampered' with, an accusation he was to level against several witnesses.

Eliza Chestney arrived at the court reclining on a specially constructed couch. Pale but composed, she received obvious sympathy as she firmly stated her belief that the man who had shot her was Rush, adding, 'I had no doubt in my mind about it,' and, 'He had a wig on and something over his face.'

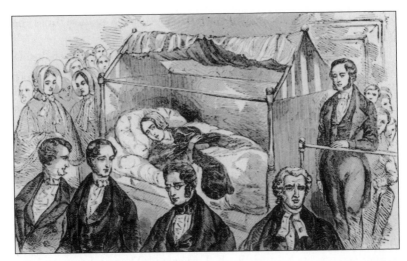

Figure 2.7. Eliza Chestney at Rush's trial.

Rush's cross examination of Chestney was ineffective. As far as the witness was concerned a covered face and head was no bar to recognising the heavy, slightly one-sided build of James Rush.

Mrs Sophia Jermy Jermy was not called by the prosecution, an advantage to Rush that he was to throw away.

Emily Sandford appeared under the supervision of the Matron of the Wymondham Bridewell looking nervous and distressed. She had been confined in the Bridewell after failing to find the 'necessary sureties' to ensure her attendance at the trial. In February she had given birth to a daughter in the Bridewell.

Sandford said that Rush had left Potash Farm on several evenings in November saying he was looking for poachers, which he had never done before that month, and on the evening of the murder he had again left for an hour or more, returning about nine or half-past nine o'clock. She

Figure 2.8. Emily Sandford at the trial accompanied by the Bridewell Matron.

said she had signed documents on Rush's instructions not understanding their content.

Rush began his cross examination of Emily Sandford by saying he wished her to understand that he was not guilty, earning a rebuke from the Judge who acidly informed him that the jury would decide that point.

Rush became excited and exclaimed, 'I feel it my duty to tell the witness I am innocent.'

The exasperated Judge replied, 'You are acting most improperly and doing yourself harm.'

The cross examination that followed was more personal than related to the murder charge and it gradually reduced Sandford to a state of weeping resignation, at which point the Judge intervened and warned that he would

Figure 2.9. Note dropped by the murderer: compare disguised writing with normal writing of Rush in Figure 2.10.

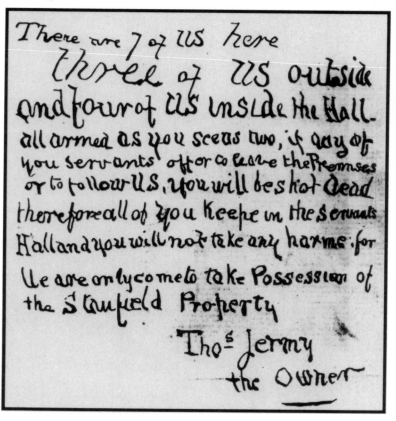

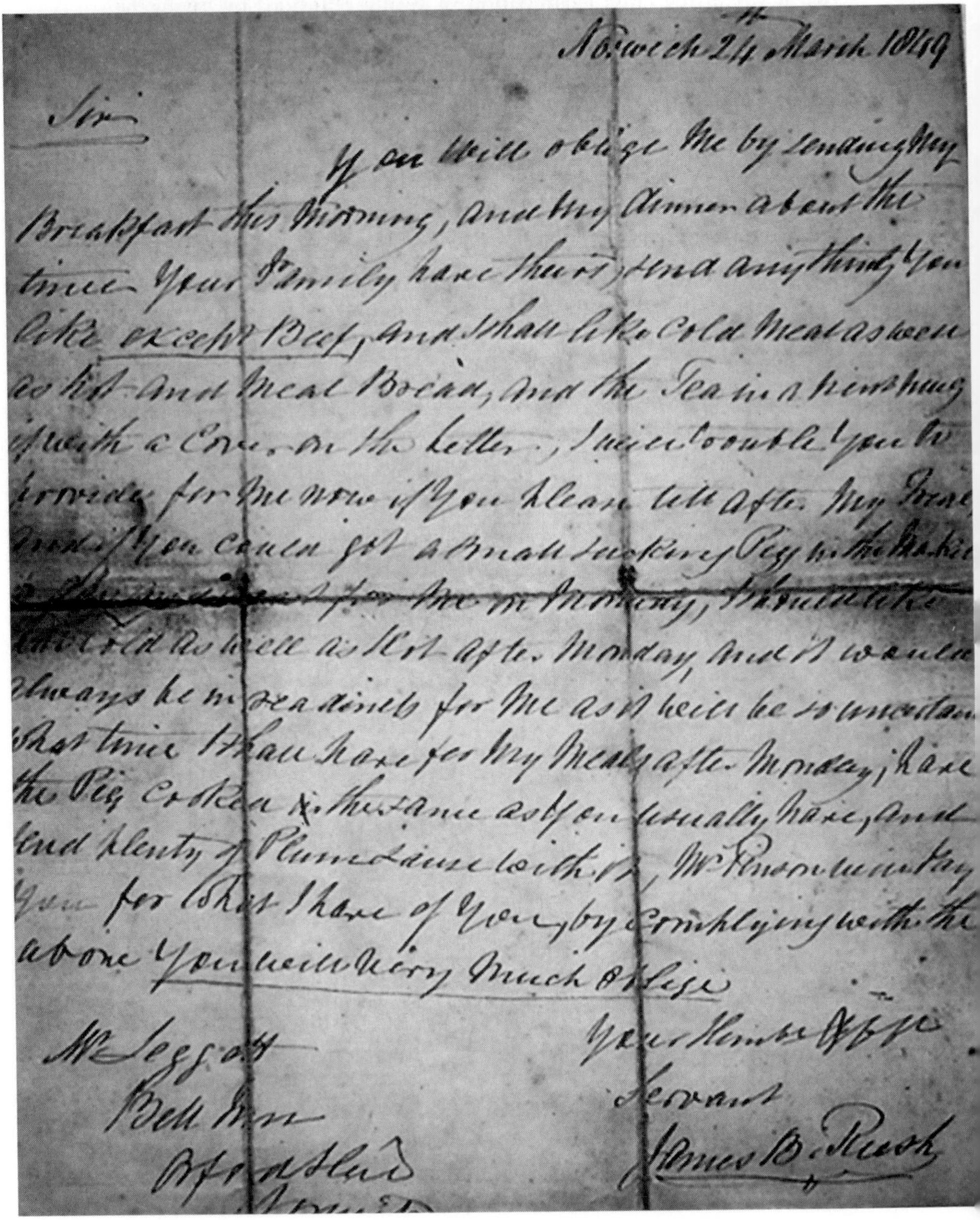

Figure 2.10. Letter written by Rush at Norwich Castle whilst awaiting trial, directed to the landlord of the Bell Inn; an arrogantly couched request for the supply of food including 'a suckling pig' from Norwich Market. Norfolk Record Office

not allow Rush to 'wound the feelings' of the young woman with questions that had no bearing on the case. There were further exchanges between Rush and Sandford, and Rush and the Judge, and feelings in the Court leant towards the weeping woman.

In one such exchange Rush told the Judge, 'I am sure her feelings have been worked upon' and she called out, 'No, my feelings have not been worked upon, only by your conduct.'

A witness who had worked with Rush when he was an auctioneer, stated that the documents found under the floorboards at Potash Farm were in Rush's handwriting and the notes dropped at Stanfield Hall by the murderer had identifying features consistent with Rush attempting to disguise his handwriting. The purported author of the notes, Thomas Jermy, confirmed that he was illiterate.

Thomas Jarrold, a bookseller from Norwich, gave evidence that the notes came from the cover of an account book sold by him to Rush.

The surgeons gave evidence of the wounds suffered by the deceased and opined a blunderbuss as the likely weapon. No such weapon had been found.

Nearly all the witnesses suffered a rambling and accusatory cross examination, which on occasions riled the Judge, causing him to threaten removal of the prisoner from the Court. Rush argued with the Judge and appeared to have perfected an art of antagonism.

Rush's defence speech to the Court lasted nearly fourteen hours, the Court sitting to eight o'clock one evening. He was dismissive of his interest in the Recorder being at home on the day of the murder, for he had business to conduct with him. The straw path he explained as a measure to dilute the trepidations of rampaging pigs.

He said he hadn't forged the mortgage documents. He had told John Cann of his other papers under the floorboards at Potash Farm and Cann had put the forged documents with them.

Rush said he knew of 'certain parties who had expressed their determination to take possession of Stanfield Hall' with the assistance of 'seven or eight men' and who had reconnoitred the Hall on the Friday before the murders. He handed a statement to the Judge, part of which the Judge read to the Court. It said that Rush knew these men as 'Joe, Dick and the lawyer'.

Rush said that on the night of the murders he had a presentiment and went as far as the boundary of Stanfield Hall where he felt ill and could go no further. He heard shots and the alarm bell ringing and returned to Potash Farm.

He dismissed the handwriting evidence by saying that the witness was a 'shrivelled-up wretch' who couldn't possibly recognise his handwriting.

He reiterated that witnesses had been turned against him and said the wig found in Potash Farm was there because he had lost his hair, but it had now grown again.

He said the witnesses to his identity as the murderer were mistaken. He then made a big mistake. He criticised the evidence of Mrs Sophia Jermy Jermy, who had not given that evidence at the trial. The Judge reminded him of this fact and asked if he wanted her deposition read, warning that it could tell against him. Rush said that he did. Her evidence, in which she said she was 'struck immediately' that the gunman was Rush, was read. Rush harangued this additional evidence against him without effect.

Then Rush made an astounding statement. He said that no person had brought forward the 'dress' he had worn on the night of the murder, along which he always wore slip shoes, and he could now reveal that, knowing he would be suspected, he had buried this 'dress' in the yard. This caused a sensation in Court and puzzled the Judge no end. It remains just as puzzling today. A note found at Potash Farm explains the statement but not the reasoning. It reads:

> As soon as Miss Sandford was in her room I went down in my slip shoes and took my outside dress and my boots and hid them in the muck in the shed ... it is most material that these things should not be discovered until after the evidence is all against me, because that outside dress will completely clear me as not being the person seen in the Hall the night after the murder, and yet it is almost as important the parties I have described should be made out – which I have no doubt can be done.

The dress and boots were found as described, but why they might have stood in Rush's favour is something only he understood. And why this convoluted note was not discovered earlier, or if it was, not declared, is also unexplained. It could only have been written, and the objects buried, in the time between the murder and the police surrounding Potash Farm. And the dress? Apparently Rush had acquired a full length widow's dress, black and all-enveloping, and he sometimes wore this in Potash Farm and the nearby area. These weird circumstances did not come within the remit of the trial. Rush had already literally talked himself to death. But he was unwise to refer to things in muck in sheds – as will be seen.

Rush concluded his address to a now weary Court by saying that he had no doubt the 'real perpetrators of the murder will be discovered' and the 'wise and understanding hearts' of the jury would give him justice for the sake of his dear children.

The Judge summed up what he called a 'protracted trial' and the jury retired. Some accounts say the jury returned after ten minutes and some record six minutes.

The verdict was 'Guilty'.

The Judge's sentencing address to Rush included these scathing words: 'there is no one that has witnessed your conduct during the trial, and heard the evidence disclosed against you, that will not feel with me, when I tell you that you must quit this world by an ignominious death, an object of unmitigated abhorrence to everyone.' With the black cap upon his head he solemnly committed Rush to be taken to a place of execution and hanged by the neck until dead.

Rush appeared stupefied. A touch on his arm led him from the dock.

There were attempts to obtain a commutation of the sentence. The *Norfolk News* thought repentance was a better solution and an execution was an 'outrage on public decency'. A petition to commute floundered.

The execution was set for twelve noon, Saturday, 21 April at Norwich Castle. The city Magistrates applied to the Home Secretary to put it back to the Monday because Saturday was market day. He declined to do so.

Rush saw his family at the castle on the Monday amid 'great lamentations' and his eldest son, also named James, later in the week.

On the Saturday horse-drawn transport of all descriptions mixed with a swelling mass of pedestrians, some of whom had risen in the middle of the night to walk great distances, all converging along roads and tracks into the city. People came from adjoining counties, from London and the north of England, determined to view the main event of the day.

Trains steaming into Thorpe Station were met by the City Police and a few miles up the line, at Attleborough, a gang of London pickpockets, known as 'The Swell Mob' were intercepted by London and local police and put on the return train. Policemen were grouped at strategic points around the castle and sixty officers lined the dry moat beneath the Castle Bridge where an ungainly and rickety scaffold (described as 'the work of an unskilled man') had been erected.

The ever-growing boisterous crowd, estimated to be over 13,000, consisted of men, women and children jostling for the best views, pedlars of ballads and broadsheets describing Rush and the murders in lurid detail, and various street sellers. Everybody wanted to know whether there was a confession: there wasn't.

At twelve o'clock Rush appeared, freshly pinioned and looking 'melancholy and dejected', the bell of St Peter Mancroft tolling a mournful rhythm. He walked steadily the sixty yards to the scaffold, accompanied by the Prison Governor and the Chaplain reciting the benediction, trailed by other officials. At the foot of the scaffold Rush trembled and raised his head to the sky.

Climbing the scaffold Rush turned his back on the crowd and said to the executioner, William Calcraft, 'For God's sake give me rope enough.' The cap was drawn over his face.

The bolt was withdrawn and Rush dropped to jeers, cheers and a solitary scream from the crowd. The black flag flew over the castle as the body twitched and became motionless. It stayed in place for the customary hour, watched by many reluctant to leave the sombre scene.

At one o'clock the body was placed in a coffin and taken into the castle for the inquest and a cast to be taken of the head (still in Norwich Castle). James Blomfield Rush was buried in the grounds of the castle, soon to return in spirit to the discomfit of some.

On Saturday, 19 May 1849, a young labourer named Burgess raked over a heap of muck in a shed at the back of Potash Farm and retrieved

Figure 2.11. The Norfolk Chronicle *depicts the hanging of Rush.* Archant

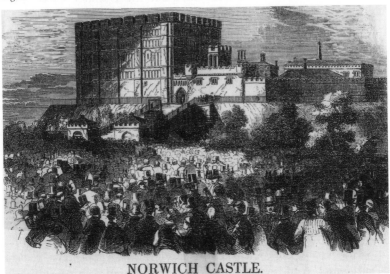

NORWICH CASTLE.

a blunderbuss. The ramrod was missing. The shed was alongside the route Rush walked on the night of the murders.

Burgess gave the blunderbuss to James Rush, son of James Blomfield Rush and current occupier of Potash Farm. Colonel Oakes, Chief Constable, heard of the discovery and sent Inspector Rose and Constable Pont to collect the weapon. Rush refused to hand it over and they took it by force. Rush immediately went to Magistrate William Cann and he sent for the officers, ordering that they give the weapon to his son, Clerk of the Justices John Cann, to be available if the Chief Constable wished to view it. They complied and reported back to the Chief Constable.

Figure 2.12. Norwich Castle retains his death mask. Norfolk Museums & Archaeology Services

On the Monday Colonel Oakes stormed into John Cann's office and demanded the blunderbuss. Cann refused and police records refer to an 'altercation' in which the Chief Constable flung open the window and called on Constable Pont to take Cann into custody. The Chief Constable then took the blunderbuss by force and searched the office, taking possession of the ramrod found at Stanfield Hall. What he didn't tell Cann until later was that he was in possession of a Sheriff's warrant.

In the furore that followed, locally and nationally, Colonel Oakes wrote to *The Times*, 'I could not otherwise be alive to the very great probability of its [blunderbuss] falling into the hands of those whose first impulse would point to the destruction of such incontestable proof of guilt.'

William and John Cann charged the Chief Constable with 'being disrespectful to Magistrates'. Another Magistrate, the Reverend Postle, supported the charge. With the Home Secretary's approval a Committee of Inquiry of some standing was formed. It included two Lords, two Baronets and a Knight of the Realm. Further charges were added by John Cann, inspired by a disaffected Superintendent Hubbersty, to the effect that the Chief Constable had 'tampered' with and 'intimidated' a witness to influence his evidence, namely Constable George Pont.

The Committee of Inquiry noted that John Cann had offered considerable obstruction to the Chief Constable and 'not in the most temperate or becoming manner'. They found no basis for any of the charges and exonerated the Chief Constable. The Home Secretary wrote that he was relieved that Colonel Oakes had been 'relieved of all imputation'.

In January 1852, Hubbersty, now an ex-Superintendent, called for a vote of no confidence in Colonel Oakes. It was defeated by sixty-five votes to seven. In June of that year the Chief Constable resigned calling attention to the opposition of a 'few individuals'.

Sophia Jermy Jermy and Eliza Chestney recovered from their wounds, though Sophia's arm had to be amputated, and Sophia married Sir Thomas Beevor with whom she had thirteen children. Eliza married a Wymondham man and they later moved to Cambridge. Emily Sandford emigrated to Australia.

James Rush junior, forced to leave Potash Farm, followed his father's career path and appeared before Magistrates for burglary and other crimes.

So many lives and careers were contaminated or destroyed by James Blomfield Rush. His notoriety endures and Norwich Castle dominates the city skyline as a reminder of his last resting place.

CHAPTER 3

A Trail of Death
The Murder of Martha
Sheward
1851

n June 1851 the *Norwich Mercury* reported 'the inhabitants of Norwich have sustained a shock of no common character', adding, 'a murder of the most brutal and atrocious kind has been committed by some fiend in the shape of humanity'. Strong words in flowery Victorian prose, entirely supported by unfolding events.

Dogs yielded the first clues. They found the first pieces of a murder victim spread widely around the city. The opening find came on Saturday, 21 June when Charles Johnson walked his dog through a narrow lane known then as Miss Martineau's Lane, now superseded by the Norwich ring road. The dog retrieved something from a plantation of trees and refused the entreaties of Johnson and the driver of a passing cart to give it up, trotting away homeward. At Johnson's home at Trowse Millgate the twin urgings of Charles Johnson and his father, Daniel, persuaded the dog to relinquish its find – a human hand, clenched with two forefingers over the thumb. Daniel Johnson took the hand to the Guildhall Police Station in a 'hamper'. The first part of the jigsaw that was Martha Sheward was in place.

Constable Daniels went to the scene of the find and the *Norfolk Chronicle* claimed there were 'thousands of people in the lane examining the locality'. Perhaps some journalistic licence here but word had quickly spread and a lot of people had turned out. They found nothing more on the Saturday.

The next morning, Captain Money, a Magistrate, ordered a 'strict search' under the command of Inspector Steward of the city police. Again the *Norfolk Chronicle* leaned toward exaggeration in reporting 'pieces of flesh brought almost hourly to the station-house, which was surrounded by crowds of people'. Reality was that Thomas Dent, a woolsorter living at Trowse Millgate, took his dog into the plantation and it retrieved a human foot, next discovering part of the side of a human body with the pelvic bone protruding. (The Norwich City Police got its own dog 108 years later.) Dent, accompanied by another man he had called over to view his finds, took the body parts to the Guildhall Police Station. The other recorded find came from Constable Futter. He found a piece of human flesh.

A theme in all that was to follow was members of the public searching for human remains upon their own initiative, and after finding them taking them to the police station. These actions, abhorrent to the present day view, have to be seen within the context of the time. Preserving the scene and bidding the police to attend was not a consideration for public or police. Neither were the police given to securing areas from public curiosity and interference. These are the facts of a long gone age. Policemen were not just untrained, they were poorly educated, little better than several of the witnesses who later made depositions and made their mark in lieu of a signature, some struggling to remember their exact age. There was no detective department or special aids and the Mayor and Magistrates dictated the course of a major crime investigation.

The population of Norwich in 1851 was 68,195, contained within a compact area that had not progressed much beyond the old city walls. A mile and a half would take a person to the extremities of the city or beyond.

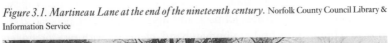

Figure 3.1. Martineau Lane at the end of the nineteenth century. Norfolk County Council Library & Information Service

Body parts began to turn up in other places, notably on the other side of the city from Miss Martineau's Lane in hedges and fields alongside the Aylsham Turnpike (Road).

On Tuesday, 24 June, Robert Leech, an iron and brass moulder, found a piece of flesh on the hedge alongside the turnpike. He delivered it to the police station and returned the next day, seemingly before the police, and found two more pieces of flesh inside the adjoining field. He again delivered them to the police station.

Next day, John Stone, a hawker, looking in a nearby field with a man named Robert Dewing, found a piece of flesh. Dewing found a human shin bone. Both men went to the Guildhall Police Station with their finds.

Accelerating gossip ensured that the Aylsham Turnpike and adjoining fields received an abundance of searchers prompted by curiosity and morbidity. Charles Johnson, fresh from the excitement of his discovery at Miss Martineau's Lane, went to the area on Thursday, 26 June and found a piece of flesh in a field. Another searcher at that time, William Neave, a baker, found part of a female breast and part of the lower body near a fence alongside the turnpike. Johnson and Neave took their finds to the police station. Constable John Flaxman found three pieces of a female breast in the same area.

Charles Grimes, a dyer's assistant, searched near the Aylsham Turnpike and found in a bordering hedge two pieces of what he called 'the belly'. He handed them to Constable Noller; perhaps he didn't want to walk to the police station. His opinion was that they had been thrown from the turnpike.

Samuel Moore of the Night Watch (untrained watchmen affiliated to the city police) searched with Constable Noller and found a bone, which he described as 'wrist to elbow', accompanied by some flesh. Moore recalled that he was not employed to search but went there on his own initiative. He waited until he came on duty that night before delivering his find to the duty Sergeant.

Ambrose Andrews, an eight-year old boy playing with other boys in a plantation at Green Hills near the Aylsham Turnpike, found three pieces of flesh. He gathered up the pieces, which he described as 'half-cooked by the heat of the sun', and took them to the police station.

Martha Sheward was coming together, slowly and anonymously. The *Norwich Mercury* described her murderer 'cutting and hacking his victim into pieces, tearing one lump from another, and then in the solitude and darkness of night – laden with his bloody spoil, prowling round the city – depositing the remains of the body he had deprived of existence in pleasant suburban walks and lonely places to be consumed by the fowls of the air or the beasts of the field'. This almost biblical passage stirred an already feverish city to further excitement. And the national press were not to be outdone. They produced lurid headlines of 'Norwich in State of Greatest Terror' and referred to 'Captain Calvert's Dragoons' being called out to contain excited crowds hampering police searches. The *Norwich Mercury* responded by complaining of the 'fabrications of persons from the Metropolis'.

Martha appeared elsewhere in the city. Charles Forster, a gardener, discovered in a field adjoining Hangman's Lane (now Heigham Road) a large piece of flesh and three smaller pieces. He gave the larger piece to a 'policeman on the spot' and, unbelievably, buried the three smaller pieces. Forster described the large piece as 'yellow with the heat of the sun' and 'from the thigh or of the belly'.

The 'policeman on the spot' may have been Constable Futter, already a finder at Miss Martineau's Lane. He took to the police station a piece of flesh he said *he* had found in the field alongside Hangman's Lane. Futter's piece was distinctive because it showed sandy coloured hair, giving rise to some coarse speculation

Figures 3.2 & 3.3. A triangle of death, mapped as open countryside in the mid-nineteenth century and seen aerially as suburban city in 2005. The Aylsham Turnpike (Road) bounds the right side of the triangle in which the remains of Martha Sheward were distributed.
Morant Maps & Mike Page Aerial Photos

from certain policemen. Futter referred to this piece as coming from 'a certain portion of the body'.

James Carter, an engine fitter, found a portion of flesh alongside the towing path at Trowse. He took it to the Guildhall Police Station and gave it to a policeman and then accompanied that policeman and grisly exhibit to the house of William Nichols, the police surgeon. After the surgeon had pronounced the flesh as human they returned to the police station where Carter laid his find 'below the steps leading to the cells' among 'other portions of a human body lying there'. Other finders also witnessed this macabre display. Martha Sheward was not being assembled in a mortuary.

Another discovery came from near Martha Sheward's home in Tabernacle Street. John Sales was employed by his father, who rejoiced in the grand title of 'Scavenger of Norwich', to clean out cockeys (ditches that were in effect sewers). In June, exact date unknown, he emptied a cockey in Bishopgate Street and noticed a quantity of blood. His father carted and laid out the contents of the cockey in Bull Close. Here, for understandable reasons, we have the exception of the police being called to the scene. Constable John Sturgess was the luckless officer.

John Sales and father sorted the soil for Constable Sturgess and revealed a piece of breast with nipple, some entrails and an unidentifiable piece of flesh. The press reported that two surgeons attended Bull Close and 'interfered' and 'cut off a portion' of the discovered remains and the police complained: an unconfirmed story. True or not, the unfortunate Constable took the body parts to the police station where he would not have been well received.

The weather at the time was described as 'excessively hot' and the discomfort caused by the reeking remains in the Guildhall, which contained civic offices and the Magistrates' Courts as well as the police station, was on the agenda when the Mayor, Henry Woodcock, Magistrates and 'Chief Constable' of Norwich City Police, Superintendent Peter Yarington, met in the building on 27 June. They began by taking evidence from three surgeons. Donald Dalrymple had singly examined the remains and again with fellow surgeons Norgate and Nichols – and they would continue to do so as further parts were discovered. Opinions given in their first statements were to be qualified by depositions many years later when the identity of the victim was known, or at least suspected. Norgate died without reaching that stage.

The surgeons identified the remains as human and female, listing a right hand, right foot, thigh bone sawn in two, a sawn part of the sacrum and similarly cut sections of the vertebrae, a pelvis sawn in half, leg and arm bones, a patella, muscle, cartilage and intestines. The surgeons agreed the dissection was crude and not the work of a practised anatomist and that the remains were of the same person. They thought the deceased had been dead a fortnight. A significant finding was that portions of the remains appeared to have been immersed in fluid. They declined to give an opinion as to which part of the body the flesh with the sandy hair came from.

Dalrymple initially refused to be drawn on the age of the deceased, beyond youngish, or her height, but years later, perhaps with hindsight, thought the deceased was about 5 feet or 5 feet 1 inch tall.

William Nichols was of the opinion the body was 'of middle stature'. He found 'evidence of youth and health at the time of death' and added that the foot and hand he examined had the appearance of a young person. He opined the age as 'under 30'. Somehow the three surgeons came up with '16 to 26 years', an opinion seized upon by the Mayor, reported by the press and later side-stepped by Dalrymple and Nichols.

The meeting resolved that placards be placed around the city, and into the county area of 'the Rural Force'. The placards are replicated below.

Supposed Murder

Several parts of a human body belonging to a person supposed to have been recently murdered, and to be that of a young female between the ages of 16 and 26 years, having been, within the last few days, found in the environs of the city of Norwich, information is requested to be given to the Chief Constable, at the Police-office, Guildhall, Norwich, of all females who may have been recently missing, together with any particulars which may lead to the detection of the person or persons who committed such supposed murder. The portions of body already found comprise the right hand and foot and several bones with numerous pieces of flesh. Further search is making for the head and remaining parts of the body.

Signed. H. Woodcock. Mayor.

The meeting also resolved that a jar and quantity of spirits of wine be obtained for preservation of the remains, to be viewed only by special order of the Magistrates.

The inhabitants of the city were stirred to continuing searches, further excited by the conclusion of the *Norwich Mercury* that 'the perpetrator

Figure 3.4. The city of Norwich in the mid-nineteenth century showing the diverse areas of disposal of Martha Sheward, (1) The Aylsham Turnpike and triangle, (2) Hangman's Lane (Heigham Road), (3) Tabernacle Street and Bishopgate Street, (4) Southgate Church Alley and (5) Martineau Lane and Trowse. Norfolk County Council Library & Information Service

Figure 3.5. Tabernacle Street, scene of dismemberment. Philip Yaxley

has not yet accomplished the disposition of all parts of the body, and is cunningly employed in tracking the steps of the searchers, becoming acquainted with the localities examined by them, and then taking his opportunity to dispose of portions of his victim in places to which examination or suspicion will not again be directed'. The newspaper based this view on the discovery of body parts in places previously searched. A counter view is that the original searches were not thorough enough.

James Palmer, a farm labourer, came up with a sinister story. Mowing in a field between the Aylsham Turnpike and Drayton Road with Christopher Cottering he saw Cottering find a thigh bone with 'a small quantity of flesh on it'. Palmer was sure the bone was not handed in to the police station. Palmer said that Cottering 'was in the habit of collecting bones to sell' and was the son of a butcher. The police only pursued this macabre tale years later when formal evidence was required, by which time Cottering and his butcher father were dead.

Southgate Church Alley provided finds in July. Henry Layton lived in the alley and worked at the nearby Albion Mills. On Saturday, 12 July, a small boy came to the Mills to report an object lying in grass next to the alley and Layton went with the boy and found a partly decomposed human foot. He took it to the Guildhall Police Station.

On 20 July Richard Fryer and Robert Field found a partly decomposed human hand in the grounds of a house adjoining Southgate Church Alley, apparently tossed over railings. The ring finger had been cut off at the second joint. Field took the hand to the Guildhall Police Station.

Martha Sheward now lay in ever-growing fragments in a pan of spirits beneath the Guildhall, known to all in the city, yet unknown. Police, public and press agonised over the unknown. How had she got in that state? And by whose hand? And who was she?

She was born Martha Francis in Norwich in 1797 and married William Sheward in 1836 at Greenwich, London. William was then aged twenty-four. That there was some incompatibility in the marriage cannot be doubted, especially in the later years, but whether she was the severely tongued harridan depicted by some researchers of this case is questionable. Certainly there are indications that Martha was strong-willed, dominant in the marriage and with few friends outside, somebody unlikely to be reported missing except by her husband, but a fairer reflection would be that Martha was strong in temperament and her husband was timid and lesser willed. Martha was a small woman, 5 feet in height, of delicate build, light complexioned with beautiful hair in golden curls described as the colour of a sovereign. A neighbour said she was 'ladylike' and a 'neat dressing person'. Her twin sister lived at Wymondham; other sisters lived in the city and at St Faiths (reached by the Aylsham Turnpike)

and a brother lived in Kings Lynn, subsequently the Norwich workhouse. A nephew lived at Thorpe.

William Sheward was small, slightly built with a quick pattering walk, a man inclined to nervousness, withdrawn and not disposed to social conversation. In 1851 he was employed at Christie's, pawnbrokers and clothiers in

Figure 3.6. Underneath the Guildhall where body parts were laid on the floor. Cells are on the left, the door to the courtroom straight ahead, and the entrance to the vaults, where the body parts were eventually buried, is top right. The author

Colegate. Before that, in 1842, he was the licensee of the *Rose Tavern* in Ber Street then a pawnbroker in St Giles Street. He went bankrupt in 1849 and the couple moved to Richmond Hill at Bracondale (close to Southgate Church Alley) and then to Tabernacle Street, a small cul-de-sac road near to Bishopgate Street. It is a supreme irony that the position of the Sheward house is a few yards from what is now the Norwich Law Courts. It is at Tabernacle Street that Martha Sheward was last seen – on 10 June 1851. From 21 June, beginning with Mr Johnson's dog, she was slowly and incompletely,

Figure 3.7. The opposite view to 3.6. After a few days the body parts were placed in a pan of spirits of wine on the floor at top left. The author

and anonymously, coming to light, retrieved as human remains fly-tipped around the city.

In addition to new portions of Martha Sheward the police station received parts of various animals, and several bloodstained items that included a sleeveless waistcoat and cotton waste found in Miss Martineau's Lane, also a bloodstained shirt found on Mousehold Heath. The police later recalled receiving these items but had no recollection of what they did with them.

The press reported several finds of bones, flesh and the like, and named several places and finders that have escaped official records. A portion of rib bones found in the river by Foundry Bridge was given publicity but never heard of again. Perhaps the press elaborated, or the police eliminated these other finds from the investigation. Animal bones brought into the police station were sifted out by the visiting surgeons, also by Sergeant Peck who had been a butcher before a policeman.

In July Superintendent Yarington told the press 'from information received the actors in this revolting murder would ere long be in the hands of justice'.

Various suspects were offered amid much public speculation. The press dubbed two old ladies as 'spiteful' when they nominated their neighbour as the murderer; and a young man who had supposedly admitted the killing was found to be the victim of his own ale inspired opinions being retold by others, suitably enhanced with each telling. Everybody had an opinion. A butcher, nominated by other regular drinkers, was taken before the Magistrates and found to be 'half-witted'. He was released.

A newly married woman living in Walworth, London, disappeared and the view was expressed, mainly by her sister, that she was the body in Norwich. The husband had Norwich connections, and he became even more of a suspect when his first, and lawful, wife turned up. Enquiries, publicity and a resurrection of the wife that wasn't, down-rated his culpability from murder to bigamy. Strangely, Walworth was in time going to provide the answer.

Relatives of missing girls came forward to promote further enquiries. Relatives of Martha Sheward did not come forward. As far as they were concerned she was not missing and in any case there was a lot of difference between sixteen to twenty-six years of age and fifty-four years. That placard was to prove a formidable obstacle. Surgeons Nichols and Dalrymple said they didn't see the placard.

As interest in the case ebbed, the theory that medical students had been rampaging through the city gained ground. A doctor from the Norfolk and Norwich Hospital wrote to the *Norfolk Chronicle* describing such a view as insulting to the medical profession.

The investigation ground to a halt, the circumstances consigned to history and gossip, Martha still openly reposing in spirits in the passage leading to the cells. Policemen came and went, retired, resigned, died – including Superintendent Yarington. On 8 June 1856 the then 'Chief Constable', Superintendent Stephen English, reported to the Watch Committee that 'remains of a female supposed to have been murdered in 1851 were still in the lower lockups and that it was desirable to have jar and contents buried'. It was agreed.

A hole was dug in a vault on the north side of the Guildhall and the remains of Martha Sheward lowered in an open vessel and covered by a bushel of lime. It is unlikely that any spiritual comfort attended her interment, the nature of which suggests that exhumation was not envisaged.

While Martha, or most of her, was still above ground in the Guildhall, William Sheward was vacating Tabernacle Street. He sold household articles and moved his furniture into rooms in St George's Street, but his tenancy there was terminated after his landlord surprised him in the company of a woman. He moved to a nearby public house and then to

King Street where he lived with Charlotte Buck. They married at Norwich Register Office on 13 February 1862. She bore him five children, some before they were married. On the marriage certificate William described himself as 'widower'. Only he knew the truth of that statement.

Enquiries made of William for his wife were met with a story that she had left him. He told one sister, who had been on poor terms with Martha, 'She can write to you if she likes' and to her brother-in-law wishing to advise her of an inheritance, 'I'll tell her when I see her'. Martha's twin sister, Mary, was the most persistent questioner but she died in November 1851 thus relieving the pressure upon William. Her husband had been present on an occasion at King Street when she demanded that William tell her where Martha had gone. William was cutting meat as Mary fired her questions and he trembled as he answered that he had walked Martha to a train and told her to write to her sisters. When it was pointed out that he was visibly shaking he declined to say anything else.

William was invited to the funeral of Martha's twin sister but said that it didn't suit him to attend. Asked if Martha could attend he replied that he was sure she could not. He was very sure.

On 22 September 1868 William Sheward purchased *The Key and Castle* public house in Oak Street. He was now comfortable in uncomfortable times, a man with a close family and an income, a man prospering and no longer subject to inquiry from his first wife's relatives; a man who had got away with murder. But by the end of 1868 he was a man in torment and 1869 was to be his nemesis.

On 1 January 1869, seventeen and a half years after the interment of a body known only to him, William Sheward was in London in a state of abject misery and confusion, tortured by his memories. At half-past ten that evening he walked into Walworth Police Station and said to Inspector James Davis of the Metropolitan Police, 'I have a charge to make against myself.' Asked to explain he hesitated before replying, 'For wilfully murdering my first wife Martha at Norwich.' He added, 'I have kept it for years. I can keep it no longer.'

Persons entering police stations to confess murders they have not committed are not unknown, then or now, and the Inspector inquired whether Sheward's mind was unsettled, suggesting that he might be suffering from delusions. The Inspector's interest sharpened when Sheward informed him that he left Norwich intending to commit suicide with the razor he had in his pocket. Inspector Davis quickly asked for and received the razor.

Sheward told the Inspector that the Almighty would not let him commit suicide and he now wished to make a written charge against himself. The Inspector wrote 'I, William Sheward of Norwich charge myself with the wilful murder of Martha Sheward, my first wife'. Sheward signed the paper and Inspector Davis counter signed. Sheward, now in great distress, moaning and sobbing, was placed in a cell.

The following morning Sheward was asked if he recalled his statement of the previous evening and he replied, 'Yes, perfectly well.'

He was then asked for 'particulars' of 'how it was done' and he replied, 'It was on 15 June 1851. I cut her throat with a razor.'

Asked, 'How was the body disposed of?' he replied, 'The body was cut up and I believe a portion is now kept in spirits of wine at the Guildhall, Norwich, by order of the Magistrates. I went last night to a house in Richmond Street, Walworth, where I first saw my first wife: that brought it so forcibly to my mind I was obliged to give myself up. You will find it is true. They will know about it in Norwich.' Pressed for further detail on the disposal of the body he replied, 'Oh don't say anymore, it's too horrible to talk about.'

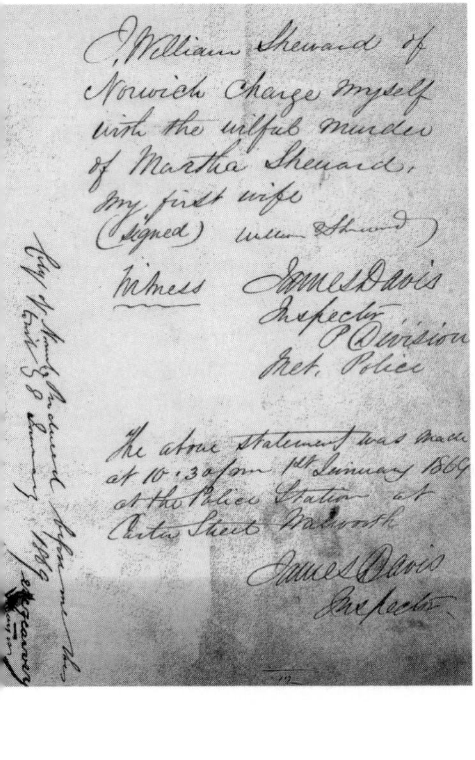
I, William Sheward of Norwich charge myself with the wilful murder of Martha Sheward, my first wife
(Signed) William Sheward
Witness James Davis Inspector P Division Met. Police

The above statement was made at 10.30 pm 1st January 1869 at the Police Station at Carter Street Walworth
James Davis Inspector

Figure 3.8. *William Sheward's confession at Walworth Police Station.* The National Archives

Inspector Davis made a deposition before a Metropolitan Magistrate on 7 January during which Sheward queried whether the Inspector was sure that he (Sheward) had charged himself with 'wilful' murder. The Inspector said he was sure and Sheward said, 'The other part is all correct.' Prisoner and Inspector travelled to Norwich that same day and on the following day, the Inspector made a deposition to Norwich Magistrates at the Guildhall.

Sheward was represented at the Norwich deposition by a solicitor, Mr Stanley, and Stanley sought to verify that his client was sober but very depressed at the time of his admission.

Inspector Davis agreed, saying, 'He was low in spirits;' (the same as Martha just below them).

Sheward was invited to make a statement but said that on the advice of Mr Stanley he would reserve his defence. He was charged with murder and committed to the Assize.

A mystery had been solved, but not officially. Nearly eighteen years on the case against William Sheward rested on a confession he was likely to withdraw, as he did. He had admitted nothing that he could not have known from information given to the public. His house at Tabernacle Street had been consistently lived in since his departure and nothing had been reported that might suggest a human body had been dissected there. And there was no proof that the body under the Guildhall was Martha, only her husband's word given in a state of severe depression. A prosecution had a long way to go.

Witnesses had to be rounded up to prove the finding of the body parts, which had to be exhumed, and the house at Tabernacle Street had to be searched. There were problems in all these areas, not least searching the house where nothing incriminating was found and the Watch Committee had to pay £3 compensation for ripping up the floorboards.

Many potential witnesses were now dead and surviving witnesses inevitably had memories clouded by time. And there was that damning placard! Medical experts had declared to the world, via the Mayor, an age of sixteen to twenty-six years. Martha Sheward was fifty-four years of age. Being missing is not the same as being dead.

The only surviving senior police officer in the case was Inspector Peck, promoted from Sergeant in 1852. (Superintendent Yarington resigned in 1851 on his appointment as Governor of the City Gaol. He died in 1852, aged forty-one years.)

Inspector Peck had been present at Martha's interment. He now supervised her return. (Peck died in August 1869, aged sixty-nine years. He had completed thirty-three years unblemished service – a rarity in times of poor discipline and short service.)

The vault containing the buried remains had been converted to a coal cellar, another indication that retrieval was not anticipated, but on 11 January 1869, in the presence of Inspector Peck and surgeons Dalrymple and Nichols, and solicitor Stanley, the remains of Martha Sheward were disinterred. Dalrymple made some blunt criticism of the method of interment and would only recognise the sawn pelvis, sacrum and vertebrae bones, saying the identity of others had been destroyed by the interment. Nichols was more forthcoming and thought all the bones he had seen nearly eighteen years before were there. Flesh and muscle from the body were, not surprisingly, no longer obvious, and one bone had escaped the containing vessel and been ruined by the lime. Inspector Peck said that he did not know who had decided upon the method of interment.

Two other surgeons, Mr Cross and Mr Cadge, called at the Guildhall to examine the remains, possibly employed by the defence though their observations were not highlighted in the trial to follow.

William Sheward was arraigned at the Norwich Assize on Monday, 29 March 1869, before Baron Pigott. He was assisted into the dock by two warders, according to the press 'overcome with emotion', but also suffering from rheumatism in his ankles. He pleaded 'Not Guilty'.

Prosecuting counsel said in his opening address, 'At the time when the prisoner made that confession, as far as outward observation could go, he was in the perfect possession of his senses and his faculties,' telling the jury, 'You have no right, in the sight of God or man, to reject that confession as untrue unless you see something in the facts inconsistent with that story.'

Defence counsel thought the jury had every right to reject the confession, saying, 'Was there anyone in the city of Norwich who could not have made the same statement if he had been subject to some delusion?'

Figure 3.9. Norwich Guildhall, where Martha Sheward lay in pieces. Norfolk County Council Library & Information Service

Prosecuting counsel anticipated the weakness of the prosecution case, dismissing the likelihood of some 'mischievous and malignant folly on the part of young medical students', claiming that bones 'sawn asunder' could not be the work of anybody acquainted with the medical profession. He told the jury, 'There is nothing inconsistent in the fact of its being the body of an old woman – the question is still perfectly open to you.'

The prosecution sought to provide a motive by calling witnesses to show that William was a man of 'dissolute habits', a man attracted to the ladies, some apparently while he was married to Martha, and there was some evidence to that effect. Witnesses were also called to show him as a husband evading questions over his wife's disappearance and apparently uncaring over her departure. But then the real fight: the medical men!

Nichols, responding to cross examination, said, 'In my judgement, the appearance of the flesh and skin was inconsistent with the woman being fifty-four years of age.' Later he achieved a balancing act by saying, 'There was nothing at all inconsistent with the opinion that the woman might be fifty-four.' Then he had another go. He said, 'I believed it to be an adult, that is between the ages of twenty-six and forty-six.' He refuted any responsibility for the sixteen to twenty-six age group displayed on the placard.

Dalrymple was on slighter better ground, giving evidence that he did not form an opinion as to 'precise age' but in cross examination saying, 'They [the remains] might be those of a person of forty or forty-five.' In re-examination he said, 'There was nothing inconsistent in the person being fifty-four.'

Another witness, a neighbour, said that Martha Sheward 'looked nearer sixty than fifty' and 'we used to call her the old lady'.

On the second day of the trial, with every space in the courtroom occupied, Sheward was again assisted into the dock. The defence made its points succinctly and forcibly.

As far as they were concerned nobody had proved that Martha Sheward was dead, and if she was it had not been proved that it was her body now in the Guildhall. Counsel went further. He said, 'They had no evidence that there was any blood in any part of the house, or his furniture, or on his clothes,' and 'it was utterly impossible that such a horrible thing could be done without leaving traces of blood behind', and 'persons who lived next door saw nothing of the prisoner going out day after day with a parcel or basket, which must have been the case if the theory of the prosecution is right', and 'the prisoner had, shortly after the alleged murder, invited people to his house in Tabernacle Street to purchase household items. They had seen nothing untoward, yet it was alleged that a body had been cut up on the premises.'

Defending counsel asked, rhetorically, where bodies dissected by medical students went, hinting darkly, that it was a 'great mystery'. The surgeons were given short shrift when he asked the jury: 'Could skilful men hesitate between twenty-six and fifty-four?'

To sow further seeds of doubt defence counsel described Martha's association with men in London, particularly her pre-marriage cohabitation with a mysterious man named Worseldine. Counsel also mentioned young women missing in Norwich in June 1851, still missing and falling neatly within the sixteen to twenty-six year age group.

His Lordship summed up with two questions already emphasised by the defence. He spoke to the jury thus: 'Was Mrs Sheward dead? Were those parts of a body found, her body? If so, there would probably not be much difficulty as to the other part of the inquiry, namely, whether the murder was committed by the prisoner.'

The jury retired at five minutes past three. They returned at twenty minutes past four with their verdict: 'Guilty'.

Sheward was asked if he had anything to say and he replied in a faint voice, 'I have nothing to say.'

The Judge, with the black cap upon his head, said, 'My painful duty is to pronounce the sentence of the law and that sentence is that you be taken hence to the place whence you came and thence to the place of execution; that you there be hanged by the neck until your body be dead; and that your body afterwards be buried within the precincts of the prison in which you shall have been last confined, and may the Lord in his mercy have compassion upon your soul.'

Sheward bowed to the Judge and was carried from the dock. It was official. The remains in the Guildhall were those of Martha Sheward.

Sheward's fate was not yet sealed. His solicitor made application to the Attorney General for a Writ of Error in respect of the trial, claiming that the Shirehall building in which the case had been heard was representative of the County of Norfolk and could not try city prisoners. That claim was rejected.

A petition, 'praying for the commutation' of Sheward's sentence, was signed by several citizens (refused by several others). It listed grounds for the Home Secretary to exert his mercy, including the length of time that had elapsed, Sheward's present peaceful family existence and the jury being of 'a class liable to be influenced by sensation'. This enraged jury members and two wrote to the press, one purporting to be on behalf of other members, reiterating their absolute conviction that Sheward was guilty.

There were more twists. Letters were received by the press in London and Norwich doubting Sheward's conviction and confirming that Worseldine, whom the defence had named as Martha Sheward's London lover, was a dubious character and had been seen in the company of an unknown woman. He was supposedly now deceased.

More sensational letters were received by the Norwich Magistrates' Clerk. They came from Martha Sheward: allegedly. The first, from Brighton, dated 31 March, signed 'A.T.', said, 'Written for Mrs Sheward at her express desire'. It claimed Martha had been 'resting satisfied of their [the jury] finding him not guilty of murder as the supposed murdered woman is now dictating this to her sole companion and attendant for the last sixteen years'. The letter claimed that Martha had returned to her 'true love', now deceased, and contained the wish that 'this strange communication can take effect without stronger proof'. Circumstances described by the writer embraced the man Worseldine without naming him. The Magistrates were unimpressed and gave the letter to Mr Stanley.

The next letter purported to come directly from Martha. It is reproduced below.

City of London, 13th April, 1869.

Gentelmen [sic] – I beg to inform you that I'm the person of Mrs Sheward and beg to Show you Still in live. In consequence I'm very ill so is impossible to write much about mine husband but I hope if God will to come to Norwich next week if the doctor allowed me and will make clear the whole affaire for the public and I hope you will make me and mine husband happy again.

I remain Gentelmen

Your obedient Servant.

MRS SHEWARD.

Can there be any doubt that this letter did come from Mrs Sheward – the second Mrs Sheward striving to save her husband's life, hoping her missive would be accepted as the work of Martha Sheward? Whether she genuinely believed in her husband's innocence is open to conjecture. If she did the belief was about to be dispelled. William Sheward confessed, and this time in detail.

Held in the prison infirmary suffering from acute rheumatism in his legs, his execution set for Monday, 19 April (changed to the 20 April because executioner William Calcraft had another appointment), William Sheward asked to see the Governor of the Norwich City Gaol in order that he might confess. His confession is reproduced below.

City Gaol, Norwich

13th April, 1869

2.45 pm

The voluntary confession of William Sheward,
under sentence of death in the above prison.

In the year 1849, in November, I placed a box of money, having £400 in it, in Mr Christie's possession for him to take care of for me. In the year 1850 to June 1851, I drew from that box £150, during which time my wife wanted me to bring the box home. Mr Christie asked me if he might make use of the money. My wife seemed then determined to fetch the box herself. I knew he could not give it to me. On the 14th June, 1851, Mr Christie asked me to go to Yarmouth, to pay £10 to a captain of a vessel laden with salt to enable him to unload on the Monday morning.

On Sunday morning, the 15th, I was going to Yarmouth on the above errand. She (my wife) said, "You shall not go; I will go to Mr Christie's and get the box of money myself, and bring it home." With that a slight altercation occurred. I ran the razor into her throat. She never spoke after. I then covered an apron over her, and went to Yarmouth. I came home at night and slept on the sofa downstairs. On the Monday I went to work and left off at four o'clock and went home. The house began to smell very faint. With that I made a fire in the bedroom and commenced to mutilate the body. Kept on until half-past nine pm. I then took some portions of the body and threw it away, arriving home at half-past ten o'clock. That night slept on the sofa again. The next day (Tuesday) went home in the afternoon about four o'clock and did the same the same night. Wednesday went to work as usual; left off early; and went home. Carried some portions in a frail basket to another part of the city. Thursday, worked the same and returned early. The head had been previously put in a saucepan and put on the fire to keep the stench away. I then broke it up and distributed it about Thorpe. Came home and emptied the pail in the cockey at Bishopgate street, with the entrails, & c. I then put the hands and feet into the same saucepan in hopes they might boil to pieces. Friday went to work, and went home early and disposed of all the remains of the body, hands and feet included, because I knew I should not be able to be at home on Saturday until late. On Sunday I burnt all the sheets, night-gown, pillow cases, and bed-tick, and all that had any blood about them. The blankets, where there were any blood on them, I rent in small pieces and distributed about the city, and made off with everything that had any blood about them. The long hair, on my return from Thorpe, I cut up with a pair of scissors into small pieces, and they blew away as I walked along. I also state I never saw of or knew my present wife until the 21st of June, 1852, twelve months after the occurrence.

I hereby give authority to place the above facts to the Home Secretary and Baron Pigott, but I request that this may not be published at present.

Taken in the presence of the undersigned the 15th day of April, 1869.

(Signed)

Wm Sheward.

J. Godwin Johnson.

Visiting Justice

Robt. Wade.

Chaplain of Norwich City Gaol

John Howarth.

Governor of the said Gaol

Can there ever have been a more terrible episode referred to as an occurrence?

On Monday, 19 April, Sheward had his last meeting with his wife. Later he wrote a letter to his wife and children asking for their forgiveness. He also wrote to Mr Stanley thanking him for 'the persevering manner' in which he conducted his defence and petition, saying, 'I am perfectly satisfied that everything that could be done was done with great ability and skill.' That evening executioner William Calcraft arrived at Norwich Thorpe Station.

At seven forty-five the following morning the prison bell tolled, joined by the bells of St Giles and St Peter Mancroft churches. Two thousand people crowded outside the prison thwarted by the first execution in the city to be held in private – if the presence of the press can be considered private.

Figure 3.10. Broadsheets pandered to a salacious public.

The Last Moments and Confession
OF
WM. SHEWARD.

On Tuesday, April 20, the last dread sentence of the law was carried out in the case of Wm. Sheward convicted at the last Norwich Assizes for the murder of his wife. The culprit died without any very painful struggles. He showed a considerable amount of nerve, although he trembled a good deal at the drop, to which he had to be carried on account of his rheumatism. In the prisoner's confession he stated that he killed his wife in June, 1851, and that he afterwards mutilated the body. He placed the head in a saucepan, and put it on the fire to keep the stench away. He then broke it up, and distributed it about Thorpe. He then put the hands and feet in the same saucepan, in hopes they might boil away. Carried portions of the body away in a pail and threw them in different parts of the city. The long hair on his return from Thorpe, he cut with a pair of scissors in small pieces and they blew away as he walked. The blankets, where there was any blood he cut in small pieces, and distributed them about the city, and made off with anything that had the appearance of blood about them. The prisoner also stated that he never saw or knew his present wife until June 21, 1852, twelve months after the occurrence,—The confession was taken in the presence of a magistrate, and the governor and chaplain.

I am a sad and wretched man,
  Borne down in care and woe,
I am doomed to die for a murder done
  Near eighteen years ago ;
A dreadful deed, as you may read,
  I long kept in my breast,
I'had no comfort day or night,
  Until I did confess.

With the dreadful knife I slew my wife,
  And her body round did throw,
Now I must die for a murder done,
  Near eighteen years ago.

I her body into pieces cut,
  And scattered it around,
Here and there, I scarce knew where,
  I placed it on the ground.
I now must die for that foul deed,
  And in a murderer's grave lie low,
I did her kill, her blood I spilled,
  Near eighteen years ago.

I boiled her head, how sad to tell,
  I was mad without a doubt,
I threw it in the different parts,
  I placed it round about ;
Kept the secret eighteen years,
  Within my guilty breast,

And till the same I did divulge,
  I day nor night could rest.

For eighteen years, in grief and tears,
  I passed many a dreary night,
I had not one moment's happiness,
  Since I killed my own dear wife ;
At length I did confess the deed,
  For which I now must die,
For a murder eighteen years ago—
  The which I don't deny.

There was letters sent from different parts,
  To say my wife did live,
To save me from the gallows,
  But none would they believe ;
I could not from Justice flee,
  I do deserve my fate,
No pen can write, or tongue can tell,
  My sad and wretched fate.

My moments they do swiftly pass,
  I soon shall sleep below,
I done that dreadful awful deed,
  Near eighteen years ago ;
I cut and mangled that poor soul,
  My heart was flinty steel,
Her limbs and body strewed about,
  In hedges, lanes, and fields.

H. Disley, Printer, 57, High street, St. Giles, London.—W.C.

3 L 2   230

Figure 3.11. Last resting place of William Sheward. A Roman Catholic Cathedral rising as an unconscious headstone. Norfolk County Council Library & Information Service

Sheward walked from the infirmary accompanied by two warders and was met by the Under Sheriff and prison surgeon, at which point he was unable to walk further and had to be carried by warders to the pinioning room. Trembling and still supported by warders he was taken to the scaffold with the chaplain reciting the funeral service. Sheward shook hands with officials and the executioner and prayed. The cap and rope were fixed and the bolt withdrawn. Outside the prison wall the crowd watched the black flag rise to signify that Martha Sheward had found her justice.

In accordance with normal practice the body remained in place for one hour before being taken down and placed before a Coroner and jury. After the formal verdict of 'lawful killing' William Sheward was buried a short distance from the scaffold. A stone with the carved initials W S was placed in a rear wall of the prison.

Today William Sheward lies under the grounds of a Roman Catholic cathedral, built on the gaol site between 1884 and 1910.

Martha Sheward lies partly somewhere in Thorpe, according to her husband, and partly beneath the Guildhall. With the case closed, and no claims from relatives (there is no record of a death certificate) Inspector Peck would have returned her to where she had rested for nearly eighteen years. Murderer and victim are lying beneath two of the city's distinguished buildings.

Reflections upon whether such facts in the twenty-first century would see William Sheward found 'Guilty', or even charged in the first place, must be tempered by acknowledging 150 years of progress in medical research and criminal investigation. Today the police and medical profession would present a much stronger case, and it wouldn't take nearly eighteen years. The 'Tabernacle Street Murder' has to be placed within its time.

CHAPTER 4

A Blacksmith's Fury
The Murders of Henry
Bidewell and Thomas Mays
1877

Many are the motives for murder, some clearly defined, some obscure and some beyond normal belief. Sometimes the killing comes from an unfettered urge rather than a considered motive. The common law definition of murder requires malice aforethought that may be express or implied and Henry March was a murderer of the express variety, exhibiting sudden blind rage manifest from a trifle – or so it seemed. What is obvious is not always correct!

There was no mystery attached to Henry March's case, the circumstances only queried by him in part and plain for all to see. He had committed a double murder in the small market town of Wymondham and been witnessed in the act, and been quickly arrested by a Norwich City Police officer outside his normal jurisdiction; features paralleled by the Rush case twenty-nine years earlier.

Among the differences between the Wymondham double murder cases of Rush in 1848 and March in 1877 are the sinister, calculated planning of Rush to achieve property, leading to a blaze of publicity that enveloped many upper class people and intrigued historians through following centuries, contrasting with the apparent spontaneous and motiveless rage of March in a working class tragedy that grabbed headlines and then died into its own niche in local history. Common to both cases are the reputed unpleasant characters of the murderers, Henry March being as irascible and intemperate as Rush was scheming and devious. But where Rush in his proven guilt was seen to be true to character, March revealed another side and, unexpectedly, another conclusion.

Henry March was, in October 1877, fifty-nine years of age, thinly but muscularly built with a careworn face and sunken eyes, less than average height, sporting light coloured whiskers and receding hair. He was a blacksmith and had worked for Thomas Mays, a retired veterinary and farmer, for nearly thirty years. This long service fell behind his work partner, Henry Bidewell, who had worked for Mays for nearly forty years.

Bidewell was fifty-six years of age, shorter than March, inclined to corpulence, and quieter and more even tempered. He lived in Folly Lane close to his workplace, the smithy at the rear of May's house. March also lived nearby, in Pople Street, where his wife and eighteen-year-old daughter (he had a son serving in the Army) operated a small shop selling tea, tobacco and sweets.

For many years the two men worked together in some kind of tolerant relationship, but in more recent times they had become quarrelsome and passers-by often heard raised voices, termed by one eavesdropper as 'coarse wrangling'. So evident was March's bad temper Mrs Bidewell tried to persuade her husband to obtain a new post; she feared March would turn to violence. Mrs Bidewell was very perceptive.

Their employer, Thomas Mays, was seventy-six years of age, a bachelor, known and liked as a nervous and kindly man. Having retired from his veterinary practice he was looking forward to complete retirement and had advised both March and Bidewell to keep an eye out for new employment. March had received the news with ill-grace, fearing that

Figure 4.1. The home of Thomas Mays. Philip Yaxley

rather than close the business Mays intended to pass it to his longest serving employee, Bidewell. March had bitterly remarked, 'He's feathering his nest out of my bones; now I may go to the devil.' March's unhappiness may have been diluted if he had known that Mays intended to give both his blacksmiths one year's wages.

On the evening of Friday, 19 October 1877, March and Bidewell drank together in *The Three Feathers* public house without obvious argument or ill-will. On the Saturday morning they reported for work as normal. March went to Kimberley Hall to conduct a routine examination of Lord Kimberley's horses and there drank two horns of beer. Bidewell remained at the smithy, working the forge. In the house Thomas Mays laid in late because he was feeling unwell. His housekeeper, Jane Bailey, was also indisposed but her niece, Sarah Bailey, a sixteen-year-old servant girl, busied herself with duties throughout the house.

At twelve o'clock, Henry Bailey, a young lad employed on Mays' farm, passed the smithy and saw March in a 'jocular mood' and thought he was 'a little forward in drink'.

At just before twelve-thirty Sarah Bailey, working in a rear bedroom of the house, heard March loudly declaring, 'If you don't hold your tongue I'll knock you down.' She shot a glance in the direction of the smithy and that glance became a horrified stare as she saw Bidewell stooping and blowing the fire with bellows and March standing behind him with a raised iron bar. March brought the bar down across the back of Bidewell's head, pitching him forward into the coal pit. Watched by the transfixed maidservant March dropped the bar and took up the bellows, briefly working the fire before picking up the iron bar and exclaiming, 'I may as well kill you at once, as I shall have to be hung for it.'

Sarah Bailey fled from the bedroom and gasped what she had seen to her master, Thomas Mays, freshly risen and writing letters. Mays may not have appreciated the savagery of the assault through the simple message that 'March has just struck Bidewell'. He took time to put on his hat before going to the smithy, tailed by his anxious maidservant.

Entering the smithy Mays saw Bidewell's legs protruding from the coal pit. An iron bar lay nearby.

'Oh! March, what have you done?' he cried.

'Nothing,' replied March sullenly.

If Mays had withdrawn and sought help he would have lived. His decision to tend to Bidewell cost him his life. As he leant over the prone figure in the coal pit March picked up and wielded the iron bar against

Figure 4.2. View of a murder; looking from the bedroom into the smithy. Philip Yaxley

the back of his head and the old man crashed to the ground. Sarah Bailey, watching from the doorway, cried, 'March pray don't do that' and March turned and made a starting motion towards her, what she described as 'imitated running'. She fled. As she ran indoors she glanced back and saw March bring the iron bar down once more. After securing the door behind her she ran crying to her aunt, then running from the house to look for her father, John Bailey, who worked on Mays' farm.

Jane Bailey went to the bedroom window and saw legs sprawled in the smithy. She called to March, as her master had before, 'Oh! What have you done?'

March, in the act of leaving the smithy, looked up and once again replied, 'Nothing.'

Jane Bailey called, 'Where's master?'

March indicated the smithy and replied, 'He's there.'

Jane Bailey put on her outside clothes and went into the yard, arriving just after John Bailey and his son George. John Bailey had passed March in Pople Street and, newly in receipt of grave news, had made another 'what have you done' enquiry, receiving another 'nothing' reply.

Inside the smithy the Baileys came upon a horrific sight. Two men lay together, alive but with frightful injuries that even to the uneducated eye made death inevitable. A bloodied two-and-a-half-foot long iron bar lay near the bodies.

Mays, his skull smashed at the front and his brain protruding, had two further wounds to the back of his head. Medical examination would identify six separate blows. He was breathing but deeply unconscious. He lived a little over an hour.

Bidewell was terribly disfigured with his lower lip and chin cut through, the whole of his left jaw smashed, deep fractures around the left eye, which had been destroyed, and the front and left side of the skull fractured with part of the left ear hewn off. Medical examination identified seven separate blows. He was unconscious and died two hours later.

The men carried Mays into his kitchen, eventually to his bedroom. Bidewell was laid next to the bellows and later taken to his house nearby.

George Bailey ran to seek help, and to spread the news, while Henry March calmly walked along Pople Street and exchanged greetings with James Flint and George Plunkett who were building a shed. Flint called to March, 'Harry, won't you come to my roof raising?'

March wryly replied, 'I'm afraid you'll have to come to mine first.'

March went to his home and removed his working apron before strolling to *The Three Feathers* public house. After consuming a pint of beer without emotion, seemingly oblivious to a growing hubbub outside, he made his way home, the object of stares, whispers and some caution.

Caudell Clarke, Mays' surgeon, informed of terrible happenings by George Bailey, went to Mays' house with Doctor Boanerges Boast and a solicitor, Mr Pomeroy. At the same time the landlord of *The White Hart*, Henry Tunaley, similarly informed by the industrious George Bailey, drove his carriage to the County Police Station at Norwich. The police Inspector stationed at Wymondham was absent taking a sick Constable to Norwich and Constable Richard Pratt, the other officer on duty, did not come upon the news as quickly as many others in the town.

Figure 4.3. House and smithy a century later, a 1970s picture. Philip Yaxley

The shed builders, Flint and Plunkett, learning of the trauma in the smithy, and seeing March returning from the public house, entered his house with him – bravely it would seem.

Plunkett was the leading light in what followed and he opened with, 'Harry, what have you been after?'

March replied, much as before, 'I have not been after anything.'

Plunkett said, one imagines with a sorrowful shaking of the head, 'This is a rum job.'

March snapped back, 'Well, what would you do if you had to fight for your life? You stoop down and I'll show you how we went to work.'

'No, I shan't stoop down,' retorted Plunkett warily.

March was undeterred. He said, 'I'll stoop down and show you.' While stooping he said, 'I pulled some cinders onto the dustpan with a piece of iron hoop and he shoved his stern against mine, as I was stooping, and I shoved him back again. Bidewell then took a bar of iron up and struck at me. I bobbed down and it went over my head. I took the bar of iron from him and knocked him down and after that I hit him again. Then the old gentleman came in and he said, "Harry, whatever are you after. What do you want to kill the man?" Then I served him the same. Poor old fellow. I'm vexed for him.'

March then sagely observed, 'I'm afraid I shall have to be hung for it.'

He called for some beer and 'came at' Plunkett, twice, jostling and tussling but eventually subsiding when Plunkett obtained some beer through the outside throng of neighbours and spectators. The three men sat together, warily, in stilted and mournful discussion, drinking beer, in turn watched by March's sobbing wife and daughter in the background.

March offered his own comparison for what he had done. He meaningfully remarked, 'It is another Rush's job.' The others nodded and waited.

Sergeant John Scott of the Norwich City Police was off duty, if such a state ever existed in a policeman's life, and was in Wymondham in plain clothes on a permitted leave of absence. (A city policeman did not leave his city, on or off duty, without permission.) The closeness of the city meant that he was known to many people, and he could hardly fail to notice the sudden wave of activity and anxiety running through the town. Having been apprised of the incident, no doubt eagerly and with the expectation of immediate action on his part, he went to Mays' house and saw the dying man in the bedroom. Assailed on all sides with updated information he went to the home of Henry March, to the relief of Plunkett and Flint and the interest of those outside.

March greeted him with, 'You come from the city. I will go with you. I hope you won't take hold of my arm.' (The last remark could have been a genuine request or implied threat.)

Scott bluntly informed him, 'You will have to come with me up to the Bridewell on a charge of attempted murder and probably in half an hour's time on a charge of murder.' He cautioned him and March said, 'I won't say anything.'

They left together, prisoner and arresting officer, leaving two witnesses consoling two women who had moved from sobbing to hysterics. A gaping crowd hurriedly made way for them, trailing alongside with the infinite curiosity that holds the ordinary caught up in the extraordinary.

As they walked March said, 'I have been a soldier; he thought of getting the best of me; but I was before his time.' Turning to the accompanying crowd he called, 'This is a rum half-day's work.'

Scott deposited his prisoner in the Bridewell into the care of Constable Pratt, this officer now fully tuned to events. (Scott received a Merit Badge and a gratuity of £3 from the Norwich Watch Committee for his arrest. Seven years later he again strayed outside the city and at Honingham arrested a deranged man who had stabbed persons in Norwich.)

March said, 'Pratt, I want to speak to you.'

Pratt replied, 'What is it you want, Harry?'

March said, 'This is a bad job for me, and I dare say this'll be the last job that ever I shall do.'

The Deputy Chief Constable of Norfolk, Paynton Piggott, arrived to take charge, later followed by the Chief Constable, Colonel Black, alarmed by a double murder and suggestions that Wymondham had been left unprotected.

March told Piggott, 'Oh! I wish to tell the truth. I had took barrows full of cinder muck across the road and when I came back my partner was scraping it up with a piece of hoop iron – the muck from the forge – and my partner stuck his backside just where I was going to blow the fire. I merely gave him a little push, and he took and flew into a passion, and he took up a bar of iron and struck at me at my head, and I bobbed and he missed me, and I took up my fist and hit him and knocked him into the coal bin; and I then picked up the bar and hit him – the same bar, the same one he struck at me – the iron bar – it's a five-eights square bar; Mr Mays came in there then – into the forge – out of his own house, and said to me, "Harry, what are you doing – you're killing the man," and he took and shoved me three yards – and struggled with me – certainly he did. He tackled me like a brick and make no mistake about it, and I hit him with my fist first, and he went down over Bidewell on the coal bin side of the bellows; and I struck him with the same bar I had hit Bidewell with – the same bar Bidewell struck at me. I had to struggle for my life because if Bidewell had hit me I should have been a dead man.'

He thought before asking, 'Are they dead? I hope not – I have no thought they should die.'

The Deputy Chief Constable replied, 'Well they are very bad.' (He knew at this time they had both died.)

March continued, 'I hope not, neither of them. As I said before God a sinner, I never had a thought, or a feeling of hurting them for the world.' At this point he burst into tears.

When questioned on his movements after the assaults he said, 'I went into the Feathers for a pint of twopenny,' adding, 'Pray God to save their lives.'

Deputy Chief Constable Piggott later explained that he did not tell March the men were dead because he did not wish to distress him further. Sergeant Scott had been more forthright.

On Monday, the Magistrates convened at the Bridewell to examine witnesses and record depositions. A solicitor, Mr S Linay, asked if he might have a watching brief on behalf of March and this was agreed.

March listened to the evidence without argument other than saying, 'The girl has said false things'. He was duly charged with the murders of Henry Bidewell and Thomas Mays and committed for trial at the Assize.

On this same day Deputy Coroner, Mr R Culley, empanelled a jury in *The White Hart* public house, walking them to the smithy under the attentive gaze of door hugging householders and a rolling phalanx of spectators. They viewed the bodies in their respective houses, Bidewell, according to reports, unrecognisable and already decomposing. Inside the forge bone fragments and a piece of Mays' hair were still visible. Bone fragments were also distributed in the parlour where Mays had first been taken. Coroner and jury filed back to *The White Hart*, still the centre of attention.

The Coroner examined witnesses, as the Magistrates had done, and eventually, at near midnight, the jury returned a verdict of wilful murder by Henry March. (He had already been charged.) This nineteenth century practice of parallel inquiries to the same end but for a different purpose has received comment in an earlier case. Time would re-order this practice into a priority sequence, each to be satisfied in their conclusions.

The trial of Henry March took place at Ipswich Winter Assize on Thursday, 1 November 1877 before Mr Justice Hawkins. March pleaded 'Not Guilty' but as he had not really disputed the facts this plea must have been motivated more by a desire to live than reliance upon a cogent defence. The Judge ordered that Mr Blofeld conduct a defence on behalf of the prisoner.

Mr Blofeld's speech emphasised the relationship of a 'good master and a good man' and queried whether malice aforethought had truly existed. He suggested that Mays might have seized the iron bar and March, fearing he was about to be attacked, might have struck back in self defence. He then switched to another defence, saying that the jury would not be able to account for the 'terrible circumstances' unless there had been some provocation. The evidence of most witnesses he left alone, but the most telling witness was of course the sixteen-year-old maidservant, Sarah Bailey, and Mr Blofeld said she was 'frightened and confused'. He finished by claiming there were 'sufficient mitigating circumstances to justify a verdict of manslaughter', beseeching the jury to return such a verdict.

The Judge began his summing up by complimenting Mr Blofeld on his able defence of the prisoner, and then proceeded to dismantle that defence. He pointed out that it was presumed that the prisoner intended the natural consequences of his acts and it was not necessary to find a motive; malice aforethought could be momentary and mitigation was a matter for Her Majesty not the jury. As for Mr Blofeld's suggestion that Mays may have seized the iron bar this had never been part of March's story. He drove the final nail home by observing that he saw no reason why Sarah Bailey should not be believed.

The jury retired for fifteen minutes before returning a 'Guilty' verdict. The Clerk of Assize formally asked March, 'What have you to say why the Court should not pronounce sentence of death upon you according to law?'

March replied, 'I have nothing to say, My Lord.'

He was formally sentenced to death, during which he stood impassively. At the conclusion he left the dock with what one observer described as a 'jaunty air'.

Mr Linay, the solicitor who had taken an interest in March's case, instituted a memorial to the Home Secretary for 'a respite of sentence' because 'the prisoner was suffering from a disorder that at times suddenly causes aberration of the mind for short periods, and the killing of Mays was wholly unpremeditated, and Bidewell's death was the result of a quarrel and the blows causing death were struck whilst the prisoner was not accountable for his actions'. Mr Linay appears to have been a man ahead of his time for within his stated grounds are the ingredients of what eighty years later would be known as 'diminished responsibility'. The Home Secretary was not impressed. He refused to commute the sentence. Henry March was doomed.

March was scheduled to hang at Norwich Castle at 8 am on Tuesday, 20 November, exactly one calendar month after his crimes. On the previous Wednesday he had his last meeting with his wife and daughter. His son, serving in the Army, did not visit but wrote his father a farewell letter.

March expressed his regret for the crimes and thanked the Governor and warders of Norwich Castle for their kindness to him. He was to be spared a public execution, such morbid and disorderly gatherings having irrevocably passed into history. Further advancement had come with only one member of the press allowed at the execution. On this occasion the selected newspaper was the *Norfolk Chronicle* and their reporter's account of Henry March's last moments is comprehensive. That report is accordingly reproduced from the point on the Saturday morning that March returned to his cell after taking Holy Communion in the Chapel.

On returning to his cell March continued his attention to the exercises of religion until ten minutes to eight o'clock, when he was removed to a room on the right of the Governor's house, and awaited the arrival of the executioner; the bell of St Peter's Mancroft meanwhile sounded his knell.

About two minutes to eight o'clock the officials and Marwood [the executioner] entered the room. Marwood forthwith proceeded to pinion the culprit, who wore his ordinary working attire, and himself assisted in the operation of pinioning without betraying the least evidence of emotion. Meanwhile, the Chaplain, who wore his surplice, had taken up his position in the Court-yard, and commenced reciting the opening sentences of the Burial Service. The pinioning having been completed, the prisoner walked firmly to the scaffold, repeating on his way after the Chaplain the Lord's Prayer, accompanied by Colonel Fitzroy, the Governor (Mr Miles J Walker), the Chief Warder, Mr Under Sheriff Hansell, Mr Haines Robinson, surgeon, Mr Hoddy, Clerk to the Visiting Justices, and the newspaper representative.

The scaffold was stationed in the paved Court-yard, behind the north face of the 'keep', at so short a distance from the pinioning room that from the commencement of the pinioning till the fall of the drop the time occupied was not more than two minutes and a half. When on the platform, after Marwood had strapped his legs, the unhappy man heaved a heavy sigh, and, with his head upturned, appeared to silently engage in prayer; but before the rope was adjusted and the cap drawn, he made a profoundly respectful bow to those present.

When all the preliminaries had been completed, Marwood disappeared from the platform, leaving on it the Governor and the head warder, one on each side of the culprit, who, however, from first to last, maintained the greatest coolness and firmness. In another instant the bolt was drawn and the culprit fell such a distance that death was instantaneous; the fact the sentence of law had duly been carried into effect being publicly notified by the hoisting of a black flag from the top of the keep.

Eventually, private executions would become truly private, ungraced by the literary skills of a witnessing journalist. But this particular reporter showed that Henry March met his end with stoicism and courage and, unlike some condemned murderers, had died instantly. William Marwood was famed for his 'long drop' method of hanging. His predecessor, William Calcraft, had favoured a short rope, which more often than not strangled in a not so quick death.

The body was left hanging for an hour before being taken down. At twelve o'clock an inquest returned a verdict of death in accordance with the law and March was buried in the castle grounds.

March left this world with a final act of contrition. A signed statement made between sentence and execution. Again, only complete replication can do justice to the document.

I had always lived on good terms with my master until last harvest. About that time the potato disease set in, and I assisted my master to take up some that had been planted in a place on which a stack had stood. We came to a place that was very wet, and all the potatoes were rotten. My master got into a great passion. After a time he said, "We shall not more than finish these today; we will take up those in the field tomorrow;" and asked me if I would help him. I said "We are very short of shoes, and I ought to be in the shop to make some." My master never spoke kindly to me after this. After harvest, in the beginning of October, I could bear it no longer, and meeting my master asked what I had done to offend him, and if I could do anything to make matters right. He said, "You remember the day we took up the potatoes, and that you refused to help me the next day; it is all over with you Harry, now." I told him I had said I only wanted to make some shoes as we had none. Shortly after he told me to look out for another place. He had bought a brickyard with a small smithy upon it, and I heard that a place was marked out for a larger one. Mr Augur, who took my master's veterinary business, went to the brickyard to give drink to a cow, and he said to the brickmaker "The smithy would make a nice shop for Harry," meaning me, "if it were a little larger." Bidewell was told of this, and accused me of trying to get the shop out of his hands, and told me that the smithy was for himself. From that time I had terrible thoughts of murdering him and my old master. I tried to get rid of them and had no thought on that morning of doing the deed five minutes before it was done. On 12th October I paid my rent to Mr Peacock. He offered to fit me up a forge in my garden, but the passage to it was too narrow for a large horse to pass through; but I mentioned it to my master. He said it would not do but if I took it he would stand at my back. I thought he said this only to keep me quiet. On the Thursday before the murder I asked my master, as I was mowing the grass plot, if he would buy a house close to Mr Augur's, if it was to be sold, and make it into a shop for me. He gave me no answer; only grumbled; and I then was certain that he would not do anything for me.

On the morning of the murder Bidewell was stooping down sweeping up the shop. He was in my way and I gave him a little push. At this he became very angry and abused me. We quarrelled for a quarter of an hour. He jeered me as he had done before about the loss of my situation, and of his now being above me. The thought came over me, "Now is the time." I seized the iron bar and struck him, and when I saw he must die I struck him again two or three times. My master came in, and all my ill-blood being up, I thought I might as well be hung for two as for one. I struck him twice. I cannot recollect striking him more. The wounds on his face were made by nails in the wall on which we hang the shoes, which cut him as he fell. Jealousy about the forge and my thinking that I was about to be cast off to get my living as I could, caused me to do the murder. I had not been drinking. I had two horns of beer at Kimberley, and I got a pint of beer on my way home after the murder. The neighbours got me another pint when I got home, but I drank but little of it.

Henry March X his mark'

So two brutal deaths were not, after all, the product of an instant, unconsidered act inspired by fleeting insanity. The fury of the blacksmith had been nurtured, a slow burning fuse waiting for inevitable unconfined rage. Two murders waiting to happen.

CHAPTER 5

Robbery with Violence
The Murder of Henry Last
1886

Saturday market day and the clamour of voices from shoppers, traders and drifters are underlined by clattering horses' hooves and rattling carriage and barrow wheels. On Saturday, 14 August 1886, the throng in Norwich city centre included a murderer looking for his predetermined victim, careless of who saw him, reckless to whom he spoke. A woman advised him that the man he wanted was not at home. He said he would return. He kept his word.

Thieves and burglars who employ violence become robbers and, to the gravest end, murderers. The extent of the violence may not be envisaged but a man who talks about his intended crime and names his victim, and openly advocates violence, is a murderer in the making. This was such a case.

This brazenly committed murder occurred during the improving years of the Norwich City Police. The force was more enlightened in the latter part of the nineteenth century, less hamstrung by overriding Magistrates but still victims of the inadequacies of the time, still devoid of proper training and beset with resignations and dismissals related to drunkenness, though there were less of them. Their public esteem was greater and the investigation of the murder of Henry Last reflected favourably upon a detective department in its infancy but, once again, there was a sting in the tail.

Henry Last was sixty-six years of age, a bachelor and retired master carpenter living alone in School Lane, a narrow lane off Bedford Street, only a few hundred yards from the main market. He was a thinly built man of quiet and retiring disposition, poorly dressed, living amidst clutter and filth (he kept pigeons in one room) and deemed to be reasonably well off because of his thrifty existence and the fact he owned and drew rent from the adjoining properties.

Between half-past ten and half-past eleven on the Saturday morning his immediate neighbour, Mrs Catherine Richmond, saw a man knock upon his door. Failing to get an answer the man spoke through her window, asking if Last was at home. She said she didn't know and the man walked away, saying, 'I'll call again.' He was carrying a wooden board and his manner was open and far removed from his intention.

Last returned home about an hour later and Mrs Richmond told him that a man had been looking for him and would call again. Last thanked her. Shortly afterwards she saw the man approach Last's door. Twenty minutes to half-an-hour later she heard Last's door bang and footsteps move quickly out of the yard.

At just before one o'clock Mrs Rachel Curl, another neighbour, went to Last's home to pay her rent. It was a good time to find the old man because he always fed the chickens in his yard precisely at one o'clock. She found the door ajar and after persistently ringing the bell went just inside the door, calling for Last. There was no answer. A heavy silence lay over the building and unfed chickens waited expectantly outside. She left, puzzled, clutching her rent money.

At around two o'clock Mrs Richmond fed the waiting chickens and wondered, but did not look for Last. Later in the afternoon another neighbour, Mrs Challis, called at Last's home and left after receiving no reply.

At eight o'clock that evening another of Last's neighbours, a young man named Henry Chilvers, perturbed by the absence of Last and a door that remained ajar, sought out Peter Hoydahl, a friend of Last. Hoydahl accompanied Chilvers to the address and went inside, seeing nothing until he obtained a light to pierce the gloom. In a small room partitioned from the main room he saw a pile of sacks and lifting them he found the body of Henry Last.

Hoydahl went to the police station at the Guildhall and returned

Figure 5.1. The home of Henry Last. Archant

with Detective Constable Beeston and Constable Hook. With the aid of an additional lamp they lifted the body and placed it on planks on a trestle, then noticing a pool of blood on the floor and wounds on the back of the head and over the right eye. Beeston found signs of a search throughout an already disordered building and returned to the police station to report his findings.

Detective Inspector Robert Mason went to the scene and on a carpenter's bench alongside the body he noted various tools and a board with a centre section freshly cut out. Hoydahl showed him a concealed safe but it was locked and a key could not be found. Upstairs Mason saw opened drawers one of which contained cigars; more cigars were scattered in the room.

HENRY LAST, THE MURDERED MAN.

Figure 5.2. Henry Last. Archant

The Police Surgeon, Doctor Robert Mills, went to the scene at midnight and concluded that death had resulted from multiple blows to the head. He found blood in dirt on the floor, around the door and mixed with dirt on the deceased's face. His later post mortem found there had been six or seven blows to the back of the head and three to the front near the eyes, some of a superficial nature but three penetrating to the brain, cracking the skull into nine pieces. He believed the injuries had been inflicted by a hammer, using the sharpened and the blunt end, and he expected the hammer to be bloodstained.

The motive for murder was clear. Property, possibly money, had been taken. But had the murderer unlocked and relocked the safe? And taken the key? Police thinking leaned towards known criminals, possibly the man seen by Mrs Richmond. The problem was she would not recognise that man again. Recognition was to come from other quarters, from a train of events in which train proved the operative word.

At around the time Henry Chilvers was seeking help to find what had happened to Henry Last an unforeseen encounter occurred at Norwich Thorpe railway station. Benjamin Munford, a warder at Norwich Castle, saw a familiar face. Local criminal George Harmer greeted Munford with

'What ho! It's better being here than up there,' unashamedly referring to the castle. He had been released at seven o'clock that morning after completing one month's hard labour for assaulting his wife. Harmer, now confronted by quizzical authority, said that his father had given him some money and he was consequently travelling to Great Yarmouth. He walked away but quickly returned to say that he was really going to the Isle of Wight. At that time he was not leaving Norwich; but it wouldn't be long.

George Harmer was twenty-six years of age, a plasterer by trade if not by inclination, described as having a pinched face, close-cropped hair, about five feet eight inches in height and of thin build – a petty thief and wife beater. He was an emotional free talking man with fewer friends than he thought he had. Following his seven o'clock release he had walked the short distance from the castle to his home at Scoles Green, a Dickensian part of the city later devastated by progress, where a neighbour, Mrs Sarah Kemp, thought he looked distraught and asked him into her house for breakfast. Harmer queried the absence of his wife, crying as Mrs Kemp read to him the farewell note left by that abused lady. Mrs Kemp gave him threepence to get a shave and a white handkerchief to replace his dirty one, and saw him go into the house of another neighbour, Mrs Mary Savage.

Mrs Savage recalled that Harmer was with her between eight and nine o'clock, constantly talking about his wife. She was to see him twice more that day, by which time he had other things on his mind.

Edward Nelson, a saw maker of Lower Westwick Street, a man with convictions for felony and poaching, was at home with his wife when Harmer arrived at about nine-thirty that morning. Harmer said he was not going to do any more work until he found his wife (he hadn't done much before) and he was going to get some money by robbing 'old Last'. It says something of Nelson's character that Harmer should have proffered him this information.

What occurred between Nelson and Harmer is Nelson's version, supported by his wife, to some extent corroborated by events. Nelson said that he tried to dissuade Harmer from robbing Last and when Harmer asked for a piece of wood and a pencil Nelson said he had neither, though he had plenty of pencils in his shop window and could easily have found some wood.

After trying to take a board from a cart Nelson was making and then attempting to appropriate Mrs Nelson's scrubbing board, denied each time, Harmer left, returning at eleven o'clock carrying a wooden board. After another abortive attempt to find a pencil he seized a metal file and

Figure 5.3. George Harmer. Archant   *Figure 5.4. Edward Nelson.* Archant

marked out the centre of the board, answering Nelson's obvious question with 'I want it to attract the old man's attention.' He showed Nelson a plasterer's hammer and said, 'I shall hit the old ———————— on the head and daze him.' Clearly the board was to be a ploy to attract the master carpenter's attention, to cause him to stoop forward to cut out the section requested by the customer. And then . . .

Harmer had not gone far for the board, a few hundred yards to the shop of James Mace, a cabinet maker of Charing Cross, where he had asked for 'a few two inch nails and a piece of wood a foot long, six inches wide and three eighths thick for Ted Nelson'. Mace had sorted out the nails and then found an odd piece of wood, Harmer saying, 'That will be about my handwriting.'

There was no shortage of sightings of Harmer between ten and eleven o'clock. Alfred Seaman, landlord of the *New Corn Exchange* public house in Bedford Street remembered him coming in and ordering threepenny worth of rum, paying with a single threepenny piece: his shaving money?

Frederick Todd, a plasterer, saw him carrying a 'piece of wood' in Bedford Street. Harmer called out and asked if Todd would treat him and Todd replied that he didn't have a farthing in his pocket. Here we have a man plotting a serious crime drinking in a public house and calling out to a friend, all within a few yards of where he intended to commit that crime, and openly carrying a board freshly obtained from Mace, seen by Nelson and Mrs Richmond, noticed by Todd, and to be found next to the body with the centre cut out.

Nelson next saw Harmer at three minutes to one, he said. Harmer was excited, shaking with beads of sweat glistening on his face and his clothes disarranged. He no longer had the board. The interchange that followed is again Nelson's version; Harmer never supplied one.

Nelson: 'What have you been doing?'

Harmer: 'I've just been and done the job, a robbing old Last.'

Nelson: 'For God's sake get off my premises.'

Harmer pulled out a white handkerchief and spread it on a box, taking from his pocket a revolver, a double barrelled pistol, a powder flask and a shot pouch, and a shut-knife and three rings, wrapping the handkerchief around them. Having secured his bundle he 'got off the premises'. Nelson claimed that Harmer was there only two minutes. The question that was never resolved is why he went there at all.

Between one and two o'clock a small group of men were hanging around near the *Bell Hotel* and any city policeman could have named them all. Harmer approached with his handkerchief bundle and motioned John Smith, a labourer, away from the group, his selection saying something about Smith's reputation. Smith's version of events would normally be treated with the same caution as that afforded to Nelson, but corroboration and his own self interest meant that his story of what followed was undeniably true. He went to Harmer's house and inspected the contents of the bundle and that afternoon he pawned the revolver and pistol in the name of John Carter. Harmer waited outside the shop. Harmer then bought a hat in a shop in Rampant Horse Street and the two men returned to Harmer's house, seen by Mrs Savage and Mrs Kemp.

Harmer now showed Smith a small box from which he took two pocket knives and two ornamental chains, putting the knives in his pocket and taking from his pockets two bunches of keys and up to twenty cigars. He gave Smith some of the cigars and the keys, 'in case he could find a lock they fitted', which again says something about Smith. Harmer produced a telescope and asked Smith to pawn it, then going upstairs and reappearing with a blanket and counterpane. The two rogues set off to another pawn shop where Harmer pawned the blanket and counterpane and Smith alias Carter was refused a pawn on the telescope. Harmer sold the powder flask and pouch from his bundle to a broker in Timberhill and used the money to retrieve a suit of clothes he had pawned almost exactly a year earlier.

Between four and five o'clock Harmer called on Mrs Kemp and Mrs Savage asking if they wanted to buy anything because he was selling up. He was wearing his retrieved suit and in Mrs Savage's words, 'was all of a shake'. The ladies didn't want to buy anything and he went away, returning with William Scott, a furniture broker of Timberhill. Scott bought all the furniture in the house.

Harmer again turned up at Mrs Savage's house. He wanted her to look after a 'box' for him. She agreed and he brought in a brown box more like a traveller's trunk. He went away but quickly returned with a 'frail basket' containing tools, which he asked her to look after. The lady again agreed, putting the basket in the box, possibly looking forward to her neighbour's departure. His next move would have encouraged that thought. He went to the railway station and an unexpected meeting with a prison warder.

The next day, Sunday 15 August, news of a city centre murder reached most ears, including Caroline Nelson, wife of Edward Nelson, who the previous day had leant an ear to her husband's conversation with Harmer. Her husband initially said that he didn't hear of the murder until the Monday when he saw posters and it was in the newspapers, but he eventually, grudgingly, admitted his wife told him on the Sunday. One can imagine some serious discussion in the Nelson household over Sunday and Monday. Going to the police with information was alien to their way of life.

On Sunday Harmer put the next stage of his plan into action. He told the accommodating Mrs Savage he was going to London to find his wife and he would write for the box to be sent on. She agreed to forward the box on receipt of his instructions and he left Norwich on the 2 pm train.

The inquest on Henry Last was formally opened on the Monday at *The Waterman's Arms* and adjourned to the next Monday. The newspapers speculated that the police had no idea who had committed the murder, true at this time, but on the following day reported that arrests had been made, also true. The police had no evidence that pointed them to the murderer but had roped in at least three suspects, one a bloodstained tramp, activity that did not go unnoticed by Edward Nelson. Mrs Savage learned of the murder but did not connect it with Harmer, she said. The murder and mystery of the locked safe, and what it may or may not contain, intrigued press and public and a small crowd lingered around School Lane on the Sunday and Monday.

George Harmer spent the Monday in London trying to sell his ill-gotten gains, drinking and seeking his wife. He told a plumber working on a house

Figure 5.5. School Lane from Bedford Street in 2005. Last lived at the far end. The author

in Battersea that he needed a drink and sold him a pearl handled knife and a ring for a shilling.

Tuesday was breakthrough day in Norwich. Edward Nelson, fearing for his future, especially if Harmer was arrested, went to the Guildhall Police Station and told as much as he thought he could afford to tell. His explanation for not going to the police on the Monday was that he didn't believe Harmer had committed the murder; and the reason he did go on the Tuesday, he said, was that 'innocent people were being taken'.

Tuesday was a vital day in other respects. Mrs Savage received a letter from Harmer requesting his box be forwarded to 'George Smith' at Wandsworth Street railway station, to be called for. For an unexplained reason she burnt the letter. Her husband bound the box and labelled it as instructed and with his wife took it to Norwich Thorpe Station. They returned home to find the police in Scoles Green.

At nine o'clock that evening Detective Inspector Mason made haste to Norwich Thorpe Station to locate the box addressed: 'Mr George Smith, Wandsworth Road railway station, Battersea, S.W.' He immediately reported to the Chief Constable, Robert Hitchman, and was instructed to follow the box. It is interesting to note that Norwich now had a Chief Constable rank (from 1859) as opposed to a Superintendent carrying the honorary title, and that the Chief Constable was giving operational orders that in earlier years a Magistrate would have given. The box was placed on the night mail train under the eagle eye of Inspector Mason, and the Chief Constable telegraphed the Metropolitan Police with details of the impending arrival of both.

At three-twenty on the Wednesday morning the night mail pulled into Liverpool Street station with Inspector Mason and box on board, to be met by detectives of the Metropolitan Police. Mason remained in the station parcels' office until the box was placed on a train to Wandsworth Road station, putting himself on the same train and following the box into the parcels' office at that station. He remained there with a London detective until midnight, then leaving to go to Scotland Yard but, as policemen the world over will confirm, as soon as you leave a long and tedious observation something happens. Somebody came for the box – and it wasn't Harmer.

On Tuesday evening, as Inspector Mason was speeding towards London on the night mail, Harmer was in lodgings in Clapham. He told his landlady, Mrs Rachel Dale, that he was from Southampton, which she immediately disbelieved on account of his strong Norfolk accent and a letter he produced postmarked 'Norwich'. On the Wednesday morning, while the Inspector watched and waited in Wandsworth Road parcels' office, Harmer confided to his landlady that he had a box 'coming up from the country' in the name of Smith. He then launched into a story of getting into a scrape by fighting and having to flee to London, none of which the woman believed. Despite this, when he asked her on the Thursday morning to collect his box she agreed. She said she would get a porter to bring it to her house and Harmer quickly said, 'No, don't do that.

I might see you on the road, and then I will come and take it.' Mrs Dale agreed. Another lady doing his bidding!

At nine-thirty on the Thursday morning Mrs Dale went to the station parcels' office and asked for George Smith's box. Two Metropolitan plain clothes policemen leapt forward. After a few quickly fired questions Constable William Mewett left to fetch his Inspector from Clapham Police Station, waiting outside the railway station as the Inspector hurried inside.

Not far from the railway station another Metropolitan Police observation existed, also designed to detain Harmer. Constable George Bennett watched a house in Trollope Street attributed to Mrs Harmer, unaware of developments at the railway station. He would soon be aware.

Constable Mewett, idling outside the station, saw Mrs Dale leave followed by plain clothes officers, and saw her gesture to a man loitering nearby; that man answered Harmer's description. The Constable got to within fifty yards before Harmer realised that the purposefully striding well built man with a gleam in his eye must be a 'copper'. Harmer ran. Mewett, armed with local knowledge, ran down an adjacent street to cut him off, but Harmer, propelled on wings of fear, raced ahead pursued by the other officers in a noisy hue and cry. Harmer was lightly built and speeding well against heavily built, pounding policemen, but he made a mistake. He ran into Trollope Street.

Constable Bennett, watching nothing happen in a rain-swept street, turned towards the sound of running feet and cries of 'Stop him'. The man he was watching for was running towards him, though whether he knew that on first viewing is doubtful. Still, a running man, and a pursued man at that, has to be stopped. Harmer, conscious of the enemy behind, careless of the man ahead with an umbrella, came to an abrupt halt as the umbrella collared him. Constable Bennett reeled in his man. Later, in evidence, he laconically said of his capture, 'We had a bit of a tussle, but nothing to speak of.'

Harmer breathlessly demanded, 'What's up? What do you want me for?' An arriving, panting Constable Mewett advised, 'A serious charge.'

Taken to Clapham Police Station Harmer was confronted by Inspector Mason who opened with 'You know me.'

Harmer replied, 'Yes.'

Mason informed him that he was being taken to Norwich on suspicion of murdering Henry Last, to which Harmer replied, 'I know nothing about it.'

Mason opened the George Smith box at the police station (if he hadn't carefully done so before) and discovered a basket of tools and Harmer's

Figure 5.6. The umbrella assisted arrest in London of a Norwich murderer. David Rowlands

clothes worn before his change to a suit. Among the tools was a plasterer's hammer, exactly as described by the police surgeon. Forensic examination for blood, hairs, dirt etc. to connect Harmer with Last's cottage was not an available speciality in 1886 and the excitement of the discovery was to be tempered by the absence of any noticeable blood on the hammer or the clothes.

Harmer was allowed to see his wife at the police station and he told her he was running away because he owed money. (At his subsequent committal his solicitor suggested he might have been running from the police because it was raining.)

The arrest was telegraphed to Chief Constable Hitchman and the news raced through the Guildhall Police Station – and seemingly out of the police station. The *Norfolk Chronicle* produced an edition covering the arrest and the expected time of Harmer's return to the city. As detectives, Inspector Mason and Sergeant Barlow, sat with their handcuffed prisoner in the train steaming towards Norwich a crowd gathered at Norwich Thorpe Station, to be disappointed. The train stopped at Trowse, a mile from Thorpe Station, and detectives and prisoner transferred to a cab, driving into the city via Bracondale and Queens Road.

Harmer was charged with murder and remanded by Magistrates to committal proceedings the next Thursday, a date published and widely noted. A large crowd surrounded the Guildhall at the time of his scheduled appearance, to be again disappointed. He had been brought from Norwich Castle by cab an hour earlier.

Harmer was not disposed to help the police with their enquiries. He quite simply said he 'didn't do it' and was at Ashby all day on the Saturday, ignoring or forgetting the people who had seen him in Norwich on that day. Those who had seen him with a board identified the cut-out board found near the body.

With the resumption of the adjourned inquest we enter the familiar situation where witnesses are traded between two courts of inquiry. But in this latter part of the century there was a glimmer of progress. The Deputy Coroner, Mr H J Mills, said that for the purpose of saving time he would 'adduce evidence already given by witnesses before Magistrates'. Here was a forward looking man. He adjourned the inquest when a juryman fainted over details of Last's injuries.

Appearing before the Magistrates, Edward Nelson was shown the plasterer's hammer found in Harmer's box and he said it was like the one Harmer had shown him.

The Chairman said, 'It may have been the one.'

Nelson replied, 'No, it was a plasterer's hammer, but a little longer on the thin part than this one.' If Nelson was right the police did not have the murder weapon. Nelson did recognise the revolver pawned in the name of John Carter, also recognised by Henry Chilvers because he owned it. He had given it to Last to sell for him.

Shopkeepers, pawnbrokers and individuals receiving articles from Harmer were not able to identity Harmer or John Smith, but Harmer had given his Scoles Green address when selling the powder flask and pouch, and John Smith, learning that the police were looking for him, came forward to hand over a pawn ticket, a bunch of five or six keys and a ring of two keys. The two keys opened Last's safe, which contained two watches, a cash box and various documents.

Edward Nelson underwent severe cross examination at both inquest and committal. There was deep suspicion of his laggardly report to the police. The extent of Smith's knowledge of Harmer's crime also came under scrutiny, though the Chairman of the Magistrates was less than subtle with some of his questions.

Chairman: 'Do you know the witness Nelson?'

Smith: 'Yes sir.'

Chairman: 'When did you last see him before Saturday?'

Smith: 'I have not seen him for six months until today.'

Chairman: 'Have you been away at all?'

Smith: 'Yes.'

Chairman: 'I won't ask you where, but when did you come out?' Was there anybody present who didn't then know where Smith had been?

Smith said he 'came out' the Wednesday before the murder, and he had no idea where Harmer had obtained the articles that were sold and pawned.

The examining Magistrates committed Harmer to the Assize charged with murder and the inquest returned a corresponding verdict: two formal inquiries with different objectives running on tram lines to one result.

The Assize in November listed three murders and a number of other crimes of violence and was dubbed the 'black assize' by the *Norfolk Chronicle*. Mr Justice Field called the list 'a very bad one' and told the Grand Jury he would review the two murder cases in Norwich, starting with the murder of a 'poor old man'. He said the evidence against Harmer was circumstantial but pointed strongly to him having committed the crime and he didn't think the jury would have any reasonable doubt in their minds in finding a 'true bill'. He then trawled through the evidence and said they would hear from 'a remarkable witness who had recently been in trouble himself'. He told the jury the police had acted with promptitude, energy and skill. He had summed up the evidence before it was given, pointed to a verdict, and commended the police.

Edward Nelson again suffered a severe cross examination, particularly when his Assize evidence differed from his deposition, creating a doubt whether Harmer really had said he intended to 'daze' Last with the hammer. Nelson told the Judge, 'There is no foundation for the suggestion that I had anything to do with the matter myself or was in conspiracy with the prisoner.'

John Smith gave evidence, like Nelson in the unfamiliar role of appearing for the prosecution, and drew more suspicion than criticism. The defence did not dispute that he had received the safe keys from Harmer.

Harmer's counsel submitted that the jury must be convinced of the prisoner's guilt and there was no blood on the hammer or the prisoner's clothes and the witness Nelson had told different stories. And Last could have sold the revolver and the buyer could have passed it to Harmer, and likewise the keys could have come to Harmer from another. The reason Harmer had not previously advanced these explanations, said his counsel, was he feared he would not be believed.

The Judge said he saw no reason why Nelson should not be believed and it would be remarkable if someone else had robbed Last after the prisoner had said he was going to rob him. He pointed out the identifications in Norwich on the day Harmer claimed he was in Ashby, the evidence of the cut-out board, the revolver and the keys that fitted the safe.

As the Clerk of the Court ordered the jury to retire and consider their verdict Harmer said, 'May I speak, sir?'

The Judge answered, 'No, not now. If you had asked me after learned counsel had finished I would have let you, but you cannot now.'

The jury retired and were back within ten minutes, but before their verdict was delivered the Judge told Harmer he had been made aware of what he wished to say and it would be of no advantage to him. The Clerk then asked the foreman of the jury for their verdict and it came back: 'Guilty.'

The Judge told Harmer, 'There cannot be the smallest reasonable doubt upon the evidence, and it is impossible for the jury to come to any other conclusion but that you were guilty of this foul murder.' He called it 'a crime regarded as one of the worst events which had happened in the criminal history of the city for many years'. With the black cap upon his head he sentenced Harmer to death, adding after the ritual 'may the Lord have mercy on your soul, for it is to him you must now turn.'

Harmer called out in a loud voice, 'I am not the man. I assure you I leave this dock innocent.' He was led away calling to the public gallery, 'I am innocent.'

The editorial in the *Norfolk Chronicle* did Harmer's hope of a commutation of sentence no favours. It saw no hope of 'merciful intervention', commenting that 'a murder was never perpetrated in colder blood or with a more sordid purpose', and 'there is not a single mitigating circumstance in the whole case'.

The appeal to the Home Secretary for clemency was dismissed, along with Last's reputation. It was noted that a 'career criminal had possibly come into contact' with the old man 'through transactions that were more than questionable'. Was Last a receiver of stolen goods? And known as such to Harmer? Harmer would have the last word on those questions.

Harmer was to be executed at Norwich Castle on Monday, 6 December, by James Berry, the executioner who had just had a bad year. In 1885 at

Exeter Prison he had tried three times to execute murderer John Lee and each time the trapdoor had refused to open, despite opening each time Lee stepped aside. Lee had consequently been reprieved. In the same year he had executed Robert Goodale at Norwich Castle but the drop had been such that Goodale's head had been torn from his body, causing detailed medical and legal discussion at the inquest as to whether he had been lawfully executed.

On the Friday Harmer was visited by his wife and mother-in-law and on the Saturday by his father, mother and brother and sister-in-law. Distressful scenes were noted. His attitude in his last days was described as 'docile and penitent', paying 'careful attention to the ministrations of the Chaplain'.

At ten minutes to eight on Monday the bell of St Peter Mancroft began tolling and at two minutes to the hour Berry pinioned Harmer. He submitted quietly. The procession of officials and prisoner walked little more than ten yards to the scaffold with the prisoner repeating the scriptures after the Chaplain. At the sound of eight o'clock striking Harmer said, 'Lord have mercy upon me' and on the second stroke he dropped. (The *Norwich Mercury* thought its readers should know that the drop was four feet six inches). The black flag rose above the Castle for

Figure 5.7. Norwich Castle, known inside and out by George Harmer, and to be the death of him.

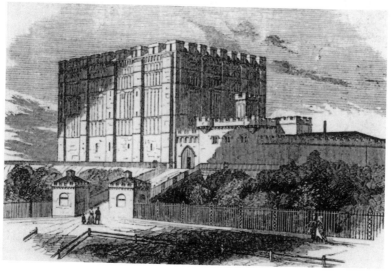

the last time, watched silently by hundreds in the Market Place and Cattle Market. The days of cheering crowds had gone, and George Harmer found his place in history as the last person to be executed at Norwich Castle.

The case was not over. Those who pondered upon Harmer's assertions of innocence and the absence of incriminating bloodstains upon his clothes and hammer, found enlightenment. The Prison Governor revealed that Harmer had made a verbal confession to a number of crimes and in respect of Henry Last had said that he intended from the outset 'to smash the old man' and 'to have no nonsense about it'. He told the Governor that he had not known Last previously and had been put up to the job by somebody else. Perhaps he gave the Governor a name.

Another revelation came after Harmer's death. Workmen clearing Last's home found a hammer under slates behind a sink. It was shown to Edward Nelson and he unhesitatingly identified it as the hammer he had seen in Harmer's possession. Did it have blood on it? It didn't matter anymore.

Edward Nelson had not finished with the case. In the Norwich Watch Committee minutes of 18 March 1887 Chief Constable Hitchman advised that Nelson had been promised some 'remuneration'. The record does not say why, or how much he was promised, but does record the Committee's authorisation for him to be paid 'expenses'. What expenses he could have incurred living only a few minutes walk from the courts we shall never know.

The redoubtable Detective Inspector Mason, already an officer with a reputation and appearing in other cases in this chronicle, went on to greater things. After joining the force in 1869 he had earned four Merit Badges, each bringing an extra sixpence per week to his pay, and for his 'great zeal and ability' in the Harmer case the Watch Committee awarded him a gratuity of three guineas. He later became Superintendent and Deputy to the Chief Constable, receiving a public testimonial in 1897 for his services to the city.

CHAPTER 6

Till Death Us Do Part
The Murder of Matilda Riches
1886

Gentleman's Walk and its extension – the Haymarket, consisted in the late nineteenth century of a straight avenue of strolling people and horse-drawn traffic bordered by shops, offices, inns, markets and cab ranks. Ornate buildings were overlooked by the stately Guildhall at The Walk end and the imperious St Peter Mancroft Church at the Haymarket end. Traders, public speakers, rioters and many others had graced or disgraced this distinguished city centre before the horror of the evening of Monday, 8 November 1886 when a man walked along Gentleman's Walk with hate in his heart and a knife in his pocket. He was looking for his wife. He found her in the Haymarket and, reckless of his and her company, and the public around him, and with little preamble, he killed her.

The press, while reporting the sudden and violent death of a thirty-year-old lady walking along a busy street in the company of another lady, were not slow to recall the murder of Henry Last a short walk from the Haymarket, his murderer still awaiting trial. The outrage over the savage death of Last mixed with amazement and shock surrounding the public death of Matilda Riches.

Some antecedents of Matilda Riches and her marriage are pertinent to her tragic end. She had been only sixteen years of age when she married Arthur Riches, six years her senior, a fish hawker from the small Suffolk town of Beccles where the couple settled, and in time the marriage faltered, the subject of much gossip, her for her supposed infidelity and extravagance and he for his undeniable quickness to temper. Arthur Riches was strongly built, hard working, determined and thrifty, but increasingly disposed to drink and of dubious character. Found in possession of a number of stolen hens he had been discharged at Quarter Sessions for a lack of evidence.

Matilda Riches was a finely built and finely dressed woman who spent money freely, mainly on clothes and drink. She earned money by taking in washing and repairing and making lace. How much her industrious side compensated for a loose way of living or how much she was unfairly the subject of gilded tales cannot be measured, but her husband clearly despaired of her profligacy and suspected her of being unfaithful.

Mrs Maria Dennington sometimes assisted Matilda with the washing and heard Arthur tell his wife in a burst of temper, 'I will be hung for you, my girl; and will swing from the bloody scaffold.' Later Mrs Dennington was treated to another outburst. She was helping with the washing when Arthur came home in a foul mood and slumped in the chair, answering his wife's solicitous greeting with, 'What have my poor old father heard about you?'

Matilda replied, 'What about?'

Her husband said, 'About that chap up the hill.' He went on to accuse her of behaving improperly and produced and opened a knife threatening to 'rip open' everything she had.

Matilda replied, 'Oh! Arthur don't; I have worked hard for them.'

He said, 'I know you have' and stormed upstairs. She followed and he shouted, 'If you come near me I will rip your bloody guts open.' They returned shortly in a more equable mood, presumably without anything being ripped open.

Two weeks before her sudden death in Norwich Matilda sold a number of articles, 'everything she could get her hands on' according to a local reporter, and left home.

Arthur Riches went to the local Rector in a condition described as 'miserable, shaky, shiftless and nerveless'. He said he wished to sign the pledge and was counselled to attend the next Temperance Society meeting. He didn't attend but on the morning of 26 October he went up to Charles Farman, the gatekeeper at Beccles railway, visibly excited, asking to be allowed to sit down. He said he had been to London to see his wife's relations (she was born in Gillingham in Suffolk) thinking his wife might be there but he had since heard she had gone to Norwich with 'that bloody fellow Larke'. He said that if he 'happened on them both together' he would forgive his wife and ask her to return home. Producing a knife, he added that if she didn't he would 'stab her, him too, and run and jump in the river and drown myself.'

He said, 'We have always lived happy and comfortable until I went home one day and found a man in my house.' Farman, somewhat alarmed,

Figure 6.1. Arthur Riches. Archant　　　　*Figure 6.2. Matilda Riches.* Archant

advised him not to go after his wife but Riches replied, 'You do not know my feelings; if I cannot live with her no other man shall.' He had a crazy expression on his face as he sharpened the knife and used it to cut his fingernails.

Arthur Riches' information concerning his wife's whereabouts was correct, certainly from 29 October when she arrived at the address of Mrs Amelia Howard in Colegate Street in the company of a man. The man asked for lodgings for Matilda for two or three days and was refused on the grounds that Mrs Howard only took 'constant lodgers'. Matilda quickly interposed saying she would have the rooms until Christmas as she and her husband were thinking of going to New Zealand at that time. She explained that her husband worked away for the railway and they had been staying together in St Stephens but she now wished to change lodgings. She introduced herself as Mrs Larke but there is no record that she introduced the man with her as her husband. It seems certain that she was changing lodgings because she correctly assumed her husband would soon know of her whereabouts at St Stephens, a more central and busy location than Colegate Street.

New lodgings were confirmed and the accompanying man, probably truly Mr Larke, went away to forever keep a low profile. Matilda obtained a job at the Swan Laundry and for just over a week she lived an uninterrupted and evenly paced life, becoming good friends with her new landlady. She

knew her husband would be looking for her and could have guessed at his
mounting anguish and temper. She had lived with him for fourteen years,
knew his mood swings, had seen the knife and heard the threats, but must
have reasoned that she would be safe in the evenings in the city centre in
the company of her landlady.

On the evening of Monday 8 November Matilda Riches and Amelia
Howard walked into the city centre. That same evening Arthur Riches
and his father, John Riches, also walked the city centre, separately and,
if John Riches is to be believed, without a common purpose or knowledge
of each other's presence.

Arthur Riches never denied that he was looking for his wife but what his
father was doing in the city was never explained. They met on Gentleman's
Walk, by accident according to John Riches. Father apparently queried
what his son was doing in Norwich, a question that was needless in the
asking and obvious in the reply – if there was one, and advised him that
he would have been better to have stayed at home. Good advice, though
the extent to which John had previously been advising and informing his
son is less laudable. John Riches knew that Matilda was in lodgings in
Norwich with a man who was not her husband, and that his son was
searching for her in an increasingly volatile state, and there can be no

*Figure 6.3. Gentleman's Walk in the nineteenth century, the castle towering in the background,
the Guildhall edging into the picture, right.* Norfolk County Council Library & Information Service

doubt that he passed on some of what he knew. Soon he would make an ill-advised comment upon the full extent of his knowledge.

Arthur and John Riches walked along Gentleman's Walk and into the Haymarket at a little after eight o'clock. Near the *Star Hotel*, opposite the Hay Hill cab rank, they came face to face with Matilda Riches and Amelia Howard. Amelia, clutching Matilda's arm, could not understand why they had come to an abrupt halt. She did not know the two men before them. Matilda, possibly encouraged by the tactile presence of Amelia, showed no fear.

There are slightly different versions of what was said between Arthur Riches and his wife. John Riches would give evidence that Arthur asked Matilda where she was going and she replied that she was going her way and he might like to do the same, a response capable of different interpretations.

Arthur undisputedly said, 'What have you been doing here?' and Matilda replied, 'I shan't tell you.'

Arthur demanded to know where his wife had got the earrings she was wearing and Amelia said they were hers and she had lent them to her friend. Arthur pulled an earring from Matilda's ear bringing a protest from Amelia.

John Riches entered the verbal fray with an observation that equated with pouring petrol on a fire, saying, 'I know more than he does about this. I know what she is doing here'.

Amelia asked Arthur Riches, with some indignation, 'Who are you, and what do you mean by insulting my friend?'

Matilda, speaking to Amelia, said, 'That is my husband.'

Her husband grabbed her and banged her head against a shop door, again demanding 'What are you doing here?' Without any reply, or time for one, he again knocked her back against the door, reaching for the brooch she was wearing, or so it was thought. His hand came up against her throat and Matilda called out, 'Oh! Mrs Howard he's got a knife.'

Amelia cried out to Arthur, 'Pray let her explain herself,' but it was too late.

Blood ran down Matilda's neck onto her jacket and onto the still clutching Amelia. John Riches seized his son's arm and was shrugged off. Matilda struggled away and into the yard of the *Star Hotel*, bringing a handkerchief to her face. Arthur came at her again, his father trying to hold him back, onlookers following into the yard and Amelia shrieking 'police'. Witnesses heard Arthur say, 'I'll be hung for you' and 'I'll kill you' as he slashed two or three times at Matilda, blood spurting from her face and neck. She gave a last cry of 'Oh!' and slumped to the ground.

Arthur Riches knelt by his stricken wife and said, 'Goodbye Matilda, I shan't see you anymore.' Standing up he said to his father, 'Take this knife,' handing over the bloodstained knife and putting blood onto his father's clothes. The crowd swarmed around the yard and a man supported Matilda, another pressing the blood soaked handkerchief against her neck. Cries of 'police, police' carried across the Haymarket and the crowd grew, craning necks for a better view of the horrific scene, parting as Constable Charles High carved his way through. The confrontation and assault could be measured more in seconds than minutes and the aftermath and removal of Arthur and Matilda Riches was almost as quick.

Constable High addressed the crowd, asking, 'Who stabbed the woman?'

Arms flung to Arthur Riches and he stepped forward, saying, 'I did,' then turning to the bloodied woman, 'I will be hung for you.'

Constable High told Arthur he was taking him into custody and received the reply 'Stop a moment.' Arthur stooped over Matilda and in a moment of melodrama shook her hand, bidding her 'goodbye'.

Men carried Matilda to the cab rank opposite, one of them staying with her as she was hauled inside the nearest cab. Amelia clambered in with her. The cab set off for the Norfolk and Norwich Hospital while Constable High propelled his unresisting prisoner to the Guildhall Police Station a short distance away.

Policemen multiplied around the scene and many witnesses faded away (as ever), but not all. Names and addresses were obtained and John Riches handed over the bloodstained knife to Detective Inspector Mason and, in his words, 'went to see if the train had gone and found it had.' The heavy clasp knife would be identified as the knife previously seen in Arthur Riches' possession.

In the cab trotting briskly towards the hospital Amelia Howard spoke frantically to the grievously injured woman and 'halfway along St Stephen's Street' heard a gurgling response, followed by silence. She presumed that Matilda had fainted but Matilda Riches had died, confirmed on arrival at the hospital.

The hospital House Surgeon, Henry Naunce, found a puncture wound on the left side of the neck about two inches below the ear, one and a half inches long and severing the external jugular vein and several branches of the carotid artery. From this wound ran a more superficial wound that appeared to have resulted from the termination of the stroke that had

Figure 6.4. The Haymarket cab rank in the 1890s. Norfolk County Council Library & Information Service

inflicted the first wound. To the left and in front of the neck was an incised wound three and three-quarter inches long that had not severed any vital organs. A more superficial wound was apparent on the left cheek and defence wounds were apparent on the fingers and thumb of one hand. The fatal blow had been the deep wound to the neck. The surgeon's opinion was that it was unlikely that anything could have been done for Matilda even if a doctor had been instantly upon the scene.

The Chief Constable, Robert Hitchman, and Police Surgeon, Robert Mills, were quickly at the hospital, just as quickly back to the police station to see the prisoner.

Sergeant Meale booked the prisoner into the police station at 8.20 pm. Riches said to him, 'If she die, I will die too. I done it in the street. I hope she will die. I gave the knife to my father.'

The Chief Constable arrived back at the station at 8.40 pm and informed Riches that his wife was dead.

Riches replied, 'I will die too. My wife left me about a fortnight ago and I came after her, and when I saw her I stabbed her.' His use of the word 'stabbed' was later to be disputed but he never disputed the remainder of that statement. He was charged with the murder of his wife.

The following day, Tuesday, curious onlookers gathered in the Haymarket to dwell over clearly visible blood, seeking and recounting as much gory information as possible and, in the manner of such events, garnishing what they didn't know with what they thought or wished they knew. Another portion of the local population crowded at the doors of the Guildhall intent upon seizing the few public seats available. Those who made it inside were disappointed. The Town Clerk told the Bench he would not be ready to proceed until the afternoon, bearing in mind the offence had occurred just the previous evening.

Less than twenty-four-hours after the death there began the twin processes of inquiry, swopping witnesses and drawing the same evidence to individual ends. Arthur Riches would attend the Magistrates' examination and be entitled to cross examine witnesses or reserve his defence.

The inquest got under way first: at twelve o'clock at the Norfolk and Norwich Hospital before the City Coroner, Mr E S Bignold. Witnesses at the inquest, including John Riches, Amelia Howard and passers-by who had observed the argument and killing, gave their evidence without contention. The jury without deliberation returned a verdict that Matilda Riches had been murdered by Arthur Riches.

The Magistrates' examination at the Guildhall was a more hectic affair though the scramble to obtain entry to the public seats was well regulated by a strong force of police. The Town Clerk, Mr H B Miller, presented the case for committal.

Arthur Riches stood in the dock, composed and attentive, not legally represented and with no intention of reserving his defence, though the first dispute came from his father during Amelia Howard's evidence. He called out from the back of the Court, 'You are getting too far.' The Magistrates ordered his removal.

Arthur Riches didn't like Amelia Howard's evidence. He cross examined her over the exact words and the order they were used in their meeting in the Haymarket.

He said to her, 'What did I first say?'

Mrs Howard: 'You asked her where she got the earrings.'

Riches: 'Did she say, "What has that to do with you?" ?'.

Mrs Howard: 'I heard her say something but I did not notice what.'

Riches: 'I pulled out one of her earrings as you said it was yours.'

Mrs Howard: 'No, I caught it.'

Riches: 'I beg your pardon. I put it into your hand.'

Mrs Howard: 'No, I caught it.'

Riches: 'Did you hear me say I would cut off her bloody ears before she should wear the earrings? That was when I pulled out my knife.'

Mrs Howard: 'I did not.'

In reply to another question she was unsure whether he had taken hold of his wife's hands after the injuries had been inflicted. She 'fancied' he did.

Arthur Riches concluded this cross examination of Amelia Howard with a statement. He said, 'I swore I would cut my wife's ears off before she would wear the earrings. I did not intend to do as much as I did. I did not intend to take my wife's life away; that I will swear.'

The Chairman invited the excited prisoner to sit down and he did so, shortly to find cause for more excitement. His father was brought in to give evidence. Speaking against and for his son's life it is no surprise that John Riches was not completely forthcoming. He spoke of the meeting in the Haymarket and his son asking about the earrings and brooch his wife was wearing.

The Town Clerk asked him, 'When he tried to get the brooch did he then strike her?'

John Riches replied, 'She aggravated him.'

Town Clerk; 'How?'

'With words.'

'What words?'

John Riches replied, 'She said, "I have heard all about how you have been going on."' Nobody else heard these words. The rest of the father's evidence diluted what others had seen or heard. He said he would like the court to know more of his son's character but he was prevented from speaking further on that subject.

He said, 'I tried to do what I could to keep him from her.'

The Town Clerk asked if Arthur had got hold of his wife in the Star Yard and received the reply, 'I can't say.' John Riches gave an identical answer when asked if he could account for the blood on Matilda's throat.

Asked if his son had said 'I will be hung for her' John Riches hesitated and eventually said, 'I can't recollect.' Reminded that he had remembered that expression when questioned at the inquest, he declined to reply.

The bloodstained knife was produced and John Riches said that he had sold it to his son four years ago.

After his evidence had been read back to him John Riches said, 'He has had a trial with her in their way of life.' His son had no questions for his father.

Arthur Page, aged twenty-five years, said he saw the struggle in the Haymarket.

Arthur Riches asked him, 'Will you swear it was not inside the yard?'

Page replied, 'I saw you also in the yard.'

Riches came back at him. 'Speak the truth; don't come and swear a man's life away.' After more cross examination he dismissively said to Page, 'You saw nothing of it at all.'

Page said, in answer to the Chairman, that he couldn't identify Arthur Riches: at the inquest he had said he could.

Sergeant Meale also earned a cross examination. Riches vigorously denied he had used the word 'stabbed'. He asked if the Sergeant had written down what he had said and the Sergeant said that he had.

Riches told him, 'That is false.' He refused to accept his use of 'stabbed', ruefully commenting, 'Give a dog a bad name, and it will be sure to stick by him, and that is the case with me I suppose.'

Other witnesses escaped without cross examination and the Magistrates formally committed Arthur Riches to the next Assize.

He appeared before Mr Justice Field on 23 November, defended by Mr Grain. The trial was unusual. Mr Grain started by asking the Judge to rule the evidence of Maria Dennington and Charles Farman (witnesses to Riches' threats and possession of the knife) inadmissible, an application the Judge rejected. They and other prosecution witnesses then gave their evidence undisturbed by serious cross examination, including Amelia Howard, Arthur Page and Sergeant Meale whom Riches had challenged at committal. When it came to closing speeches prosecuting counsel said the facts had not been contested and he therefore had nothing further to say.

Mr Grain, having accepted the prosecution evidence, had to say something. He referred to a 'pathetic case' and a 'painful story' and tried to dismiss Riches' threats by saying such words used in the 'prisoner's class of life' did not mean the same as they would if used by a person in a 'higher station in life'. In his view, if the prisoner had found his wife living quietly in a house there would not have been a problem but instead he found her 'walking about with borrowed trinkets' in a part of Norwich that might be known to the jury. He suggested the intention of Riches was to cut the earrings from his wife's ears with no malice aforethought to murder. He thought that in the circumstances there was provocation and a manslaughter verdict could be considered. This provoked the Judge who demanded to know how Mr Grain could justify asking for a manslaughter verdict. Mr Grain said the evidence should be looked at narrowly, which upset the Judge some more and led to verbal exchanges on the law, which Mr Grain was bound to lose. The Judge ruled that the jury must not look at the evidence narrowly but dispassionately. He said he saw no evidence of manslaughter, which did not deter Mr Grain from doggedly closing his speech to the jury by suggesting there was no malice and no intention to kill and therefore the unlawful act was manslaughter.

The Judge summed up, speaking of a woman walking quietly along within the Queen's peace receiving three cuts across her throat. He said if there was provocation it was not grave and the initial attack had been followed up. He thought the remark of the prisoner's father, 'I know what she is doing here', was to be regretted. He told the jury there was nothing in the case to reduce the crime to manslaughter, possibly casting a keen eye at Mr Grain who had had the temerity to argue otherwise. From this point the verdict could not have been in doubt and the jury retired for only eighteen minutes. The foreman wanted to make a statement before delivering the verdict but the Judge would not allow it. The foreman responded by wrapping his statement round the verdict.

He said, 'We find him guilty of murder, but with a strong recommendation to mercy on account of great provocation.'

The Judge addressed Riches, saying the jury had no alternative but to find a verdict of murder and, whilst no one could doubt he had been badly treated, there was no justification for 'a cruel murder in which you destroyed that poor woman's life'. He said he would forward on the recommendation for mercy. With the black cap on his head he proceeded to the ritual formula of the death sentence.

During the sentencing Riches stood impassively, with folded arms. At the end he touched his forehead and said, 'Thank you, My Lord.' He was led away.

A petition to commute the sentence received signatures from the Mayor and Town Clerk of Beccles, the Norwich Magistrate who had committed Riches for trial, the foreman of the jury that had found him guilty and hundreds of citizens of the city of Norwich and counties of Norfolk and Suffolk, including a knight and others of high standing in the community. The answer came within a few days. Arthur Riches was reprieved, now sentenced to penal servitude for life.

Can there have been a case where a killer attracted so much sympathy and his victim so little? The *Norwich Mercury* celebrated with an article that concluded that Riches had been 'goaded to the murder of his wife', noting that she had been found 'bedecked in tawdry jewellery' in 'a place where women of questionable fame most do congregate'. The newspaper also sympathised with John Riches, recording that 'if the old man's memory did seem a little defective the fact was charitably overlooked as the natural desire of the father to shield his son'.

The *Norfolk Chronicle* was not so charitable, reacting to two recommendations for mercy at the same assize – the other in respect of a killing of a child by its mother at Fakenham. The newspaper claimed that in 'the class from which in the most part jurors are drawn there existed a sort of sneaking sympathy with the criminal'.

Life for Arthur Riches meant another twelve years. He died at Parkhurst Prison on the Isle of Wight in April 1898, aged forty-eight years. There was no mystery attached to his case, just the exceptional tragedy of a husband and wife, and a father and son.

CHAPTER 7

Your Days Are My Days
The Murder of Sophia Watt
1898

George and Sophia Watt married in 1876 at Norwich Registry Office but any ensuing happiness occurred in the first two years of the marriage. After twenty years of attrition Sophia applied to Norwich Magistrates for a separation order, alleging persistent cruelty. The hearing was set for 22 February 1898. Sophia had effectively ended her life.

Fearing her husband's reaction to the application, Sophia left the family home in Fishgate Street (now Fishergate) to live with a friend, Mrs Phoebe Paston, in Northcote Road; but it was not far enough and on 19 February her drunken husband forced his way inside the house triumphantly declaring 'Now I've found you.' Mrs Paston shrieked, 'Murder', a not unusual Victorian cry of alarm but in this case somewhat prescient, and sent for the police. Sergeant Martins of the city force went to the house and curbed George Watt's instinct for violence, if not his threats.

George demanded that his wife hand over money she had taken and return home, promising he would not ill-treat her again, vehemently announcing, 'Your days are my days'.

Sophia replied that she would rather go to the bottom of the river than return home with her husband, whereupon he recklessly threatened 'I shall kill you Sophie, one day I shall kill you.' Sergeant Martins led George away and recorded the incident as one of 'annoyance'.

On 22 February Sophia told the Magistrates that her husband had ill-treated her for twenty years and only recently had returned home in a bad temper and kicked her out of bed, striking her in the face and blacking both her eyes. On that occasion she had been saved from further injury by the intervention of her seventeen-year-old son, Joseph. She said that just before Christmas her husband had broken her nose and she had consequently received hospital treatment.

Sophia's eldest son, James, a twenty-three-year-old Lance Corporal in the Royal Marines, and her next eldest, Joseph, supported their mother's evidence, speaking of a history of threats and violence. James said that he had recently rushed home from Chatham after receiving an urgent telegram calling for him to protect his mother.

George Watt agreed that he had assaulted his wife but said he had not used his fist and he had been the worse for drink. He said his wife was 'very quick and sharp' and she had once broken an umbrella over his head. He said he did not want a separation and was 'an honest and upright man' earning one pound per week as a cellarman.

Sophia told the Magistrates she did not want any money from her husband in case he saw that as a hold upon her. She did ask for custody of her two youngest children, aged six and nine years (some reports vary these ages slightly), seemingly not mentioning a twelve-year-old son. (Sophia Watt had five children.)

The Magistrates made a separation order and ordered George Watt to pay five shillings per week to maintain the children, also costs of twelve shillings and sixpence.

George, disaffected and displaced from the family home, moved into lodgings in Fishgate Street and on 26 February traced his wife to her new address at Campling's Yard in St Saviour's Lane (close to Fishgate Street), pushing his way inside. He hit her on the shoulder but was then propelled outside by Joseph. Summoned before the Magistrates for breaching the separation order he was fined five shillings and warned that another occurrence would be severely dealt with. Two days later he was back at his wife's house asking her to withdraw the summons she had issued for assault. When she refused he produced a knife saying, 'If you don't I will do for you.' James Watt wrestled the knife away and received cuts to his hand in the process. The struggle continued in the yard outside, during which George called to his wife 'If it is twenty years to come I will do for you.'

Appearing again before the Magistrates, this time with a bandaged head, George said he was 'very sorry' and had gone to see his wife to ask for forgiveness. He couldn't remember what happened because he had had 'a glass or two'. The Magistrates extended him leniency because he had 'very much been knocked about' (James had more than defended his mother) and bound him to keep the peace for six months.

The problem for George Watt was there were too many times in his life when he had enjoyed a 'glass or two'. In 1898 he was aged forty-four years, a tall, wirily built man with a soldierly bearing that stemmed from twelve years' service with the Field Artillery, quiet and even tempered when sober and fiercely aggressive when not. Born in Scotland of poor parents and receiving a strict upbringing in deprived times, he had joined the Army as many of similar antecedents had done. Now he worked in a boot and shoe factory.

Sophia Watt was forty-five years of age, a local woman of strong appearance and for twenty years evidently of a forgiving nature. The mother of four of George's children (James was born through another man the year before she married George), she was supposed to have liked a drink and George thought, rightly or wrongly, that she was inclined to flirt. There can be no doubt that she had suffered at his hands and had forgiven him on numerous occasions, and was now determined to foreclose on the marriage. In late March she moved to Denmark Terrace, a row of cottages alongside Sprowston Road. Her husband soon knew of her new address, proved by the fact he sent endearing letters there, some written for him by his landlord and some by a fellow lodger.

The letters show George Watt as repentant and desperate. He was now out of work as a result of his court appearances, and his lodgings were being paid for by his brother, 'Scotty' Watt, whom George visited to obtain meals. In a letter dated 23 March, written for him by fellow lodger James Phillips, he blamed his misfortune upon 'the accursed drink' and asked his sons to forgive their 'hard father'. He vowed he would 'never taste another drop again', asking Sophia to 'give me one more chance', promising 'I will love you with kindness'. He wrote, by proxy, 'Don't be afraid of me dear' and said he had 'not had above a pennyworth of bread a day this last fortnight and some days none' and 'never again will I lift a finger to harm you'. After Phillips had concluded the letter Watt ominously commented, 'If she do not take me back she little thinks she is making orphans of the children.' Phillips took this as a contemplation of suicide.

Who delivered the letters is not known but we can be sure that they did not have the intended effect. Sophia remained steadfastly separate from her husband, not believing anything he, or anybody else, wrote. But her husband had somehow acquired some money, and while professing hunger and everlasting love for his wife he was, on 4 April, spending the princely sum of eight shillings upon a revolver and 50 cartridges. On 9 April he returned the revolver to the gunsmith because it didn't revolve. The weapon was repaired and George Watt became armed and obsessed.

On the morning of 14 April he personally wrote to his wife, keeping the letter with him, intending to make a personal delivery. He also nursed other intentions. In a mood of apparent despair he told his landlord, Frederick Edwards, he was hard-up and couldn't get work. The landlord commiserated and thought that Watt hadn't eaten that day and was sober.

At two o'clock Watt looked up at the clock in his lodgings and said, 'Oh! It's just gone two.' He left the building in the manner of a man on a mission.

At 2.30 pm, Sophia Watt in the last moments of her life stretched out a linen line in her small back yard, her young daughter playing nearby. The row of yards at the rear of Denmark Terrace overlooked each other and were accessed by a communal alley. As George Watt came into view George Drake, a shoemaker living next door to Sophia Watt, was busy in his yard workshop while another neighbour, Lily Burrows, watched George from her window. Another neighbour, Emma Girling, was busy near her window, soon to notice George.

Mrs Burrows saw the little girl run indoors as George entered the yard and she heard Sophia say, 'I expect she is afraid of you.' George said he would not hurt the girl and followed his wife along the yard. Their conversation was brief, but pointed enough to keep Mrs Burrows interested. George asked for a reconciliation and Sophia replied that she had heard his promises before and now wanted nothing more to do with him. She picked up a mat and banged it against a wall, hanging it up and dismissively walking past her husband. His hand came up; a gunshot rang out, then more shots. A horrified Mrs Burrows saw George holding a 'pistol' and firing successive shots into his wife's head. Sophia tumbled to the ground and George stooped to fire a third shot into her head.

George Drake, alerted by the shots, saw George stooping over his wife's body, firing into her head. Emma Girling, running outside her home, also saw George firing into his wife's fallen body.

All the witnesses saw George reverse the revolver and belabour his wife's head with the butt. Emma Girling said he then put the gun muzzle in his mouth but quickly withdrew it.

George Drake shouted, 'Murder! Help!' and George Watt looked up, stopped beating his wife and leapt over palings, then springing over a fence and running across a field. Drake followed him across the field and onto the Sprowston Road, running to catch up as Watt approached *The Norfolk Arms* public house. Watt stopped suddenly, turned, and took the revolver from his pocket, beckoning Drake to 'come on'. That gentleman wisely decided to hold back. Watt resumed running, carefully followed by

Drake, and disappeared inside the public house. Drake watched the front of the building while other arriving men watched the back. Another ran to fetch the police.

Inspector Flint and Sergeant Spight of the county police (Denmark Terrace was one hundred yards inside county jurisdiction) arrived at the public house in a carriage but news of the murder had travelled ahead of them, causing great excitement inside the building and Watt to dash out the rear, last seen striding out onto Mousehold Heath.

Back at Denmark Terrace Sophia was clearly dead. Horace Edwards, living nearby, was first to examine the body lying on its right side. He turned it face upwards, blood running from the head and staining an envelope and letter under an arm. He handed the envelope and letter to Constable Slater who had arrived at the scene with Constable Warnes. They covered the body with a sheet as a deterrent to faces peering into the yard but a small crowd of onlookers remained outside, several coming later to gaze at the pool of blood.

Doctor Charles Duff arrived and ordered the body to be taken into the house where he made a preliminary examination, later conducting a post-mortem.

The doctor found two bullet wounds in the left side of the head and another in the left breast, all entry wounds. A wound further back on the head he attributed to a bullet exiting having been deflected by the skull. He was to sum it up as three shots and four wounds, one bullet making two wounds. The two bullets recovered from the body, one in the brain and one in the heart, would have been instantly fatal. He strangely found no wounds consistent with the head being struck by the butt of the gun.

News of the murder and details of the murderer flashed around a city that was compact, intimate and disposed to accelerating gossip and sensation. The *Eastern Evening News* helped by getting their reporter to Denmark Terrace almost as quickly as the police, producing a new edition of the newspaper within one and a half hours of the murder, describing a 'Shocking crime at Sprowston' and the wanted man by name.

The murderer evaded custody during the afternoon but there was no shortage of sightings, real or imagined. He was seen in Constitution Hill, Waterloo Road, Pitt Street, Golden Dog Lane, Fishgate Street and Peacock Street. He changed his clothes at his brother's house in the quaintly named Hen and Chickens Yard at St Mary's Plain and quickly moved on. In Peacock Street he tried to find refuge at the house of Eliza Chamberlain, a lady he knew, asking if he could come inside.

SHOCKING
MURDER
AT
SPROWSTON.

A WIFE SHOT DEAD.

TERRIBLE SCENE IN A
BACK YARD.

ASSAILANT'S ESCAPE

The parish of Sprowston was horrified this afternoon by the news of a shocking tragedy, in which a woman was shot dead under terrible circumstances. It would appear that the tragic affair occurred about half-past two o'clock this afternoon, the

Figure 7.1. Headlines that brought a murderer to book. Archant

Mrs Chamberlain exclaimed, 'No, certainly not.' She knew of the murder; most people did by now.

Watt swore, asked again and pushed the lady. She locked her door against him, crying, 'Oh Watt! What have you done?'

He replied, 'What I intended doing for months past.'

He must have known the end was near. The city buzzed with excitement. Everybody was talking about him, looking for and seeing him (truly or otherwise). Excited citizens followed him from Mrs Chamberlain's rebuttal in Peacock Street to St Saviour's Lane where he disappeared inside *The Hope Brewery* public house, leaving a growing crowd outside. The pub landlady, conscious of the agitation outside and the reason for it inside, served Watt a drink and nervously waited. He left after one drink.

A Mr Syder and a Mr Smart told the press they recognised Watt in St Saviour's Lane and offered him a cigarette, and whilst he was in their company he bought a copy of the *Evening News,* quickly reading of the murder and throwing the newspaper away. They said they walked with him into Magdalen Street and delivered him to a Constable. More general reports say that he was accompanied along Magdalen Street by a hooting, jeering crowd and Watt's son (believed the twelve-year-old) arrived and struck his father shouting, 'I'll teach you to murder my mother,' the crowd then cheering wildly, their enthusiasm becoming even greater as a Constable arrived to arrest, or rescue, the fugitive.

Constable Walter Grimes, a young officer with eight months' service, made the arrest. He handcuffed his unresisting prisoner to applause and cheers from a crowd estimated by Grimes at 600 to 700.

Figure 7.2. Peacock Street, leading to Fishgate Street (Fishergate), Norwich's Anglican Cathedral in the background. The fugitive sought and was denied refuge in this street. Norfolk County Council Library & Information Service

Watt is alleged to have told Constable Grimes 'I have got no revolver' and spoken of seeing 'three or four men' coming from his wife's house, comments that he chose not to repeat at the police station.

Inspector Flint finally faced his man at the Guildhall Police Station, informing Watt he would be charged with the murder of his wife. Watt replied, 'I know nothing about it.'

The prisoner was taken to the County Police Station at Castle Meadow and a crowd, anxious not to lose sight of sensational events, milled around outside.

Detective Sergeant Slaughter of the city force visited 'Scotty' Watt and recovered the clothes worn by George at the time of the murder and wider searches were made for the revolver, without success.

Figure 7.3. The Hope Brewery, *desolate and awaiting demolition in 1939 but once besieged by a crowd waiting for a murderer inside.* George Plunkett

Watt appeared before Magistrates at the Shirehall on the Friday and Saturday before being hurried by cab to the Norwich Prison at Plumstead Road, this establishment taking over from the City Gaol at St Giles (pulled down) and Norwich Castle (becoming a museum). On this same day the inquest opened and concluded at *The Norfolk Arms*. Eye witnesses to the murder and evidence of the turbulent history of the marriage made the jury's task straightforward. They recorded a verdict that George Watt murdered Sophia Watt. At the hearing the Coroner, Mr W Barton, disclosed the contents of the letter found under Sophia's body. James Watt identified the handwriting as that of George Watt.

The letter, dated '14.4.98', read:

My Dear Wife

I hope you and the children are in good health. I cannot say I am. Will you tell me what I am to do. You had my £4 10s and my home. You and my children gone. I have got the street. Is your heart that hard you cannot forget it? I love you with all my heart. I have got no work, no home. God bless you all. Think, no home.

G. Watt

The envelope was addressed 'Mrs Watt, Denmark Terrace, Sprowston'.

The Coroner made no comment upon this pleading communication.

A subscription fund was started to aid the dependants of Sophia Watt and to defray the cost of the funeral. The funeral procession started at eight-thirty on the morning of 18 April from Denmark Terrace with few onlookers, but the presence of a large number of policemen soon attracted a crowd estimated at 300. The cortège was initially escorted by Norfolk County Police officers, handing over to Norwich City Police officers at the city boundary only yards away, the mournful procession wending its way to Earlham Cemetery where the press reported family scenes of great distress.

Committal proceedings were delayed. The police wanted time to find the revolver; Judges had been known to become irascible over evidence adduced after the committal. But Watt had not been forthcoming and in any case he could hardly tell where he had disposed of the murder weapon if he was saying he didn't commit the murder. Searches along the route taken by the fleeing man were unsuccessful. Checking his lodgings, brother's address and the streets in which he had been seen produced no better result.

Another remand was granted, until 30 April when it seemed the committal would have to go ahead. And it did go ahead – with the revolver as an exhibit, found on 27 April. George Watt had confided in a friend, proving that bonding is better than browbeating.

John Clarke had been an official friend of George Watt before the shooting. As police court missionary (a kind of early-day probation officer) he dispensed advice and acted as counsellor in matters both criminal and distressing. He was seen as a kindly, genuine and well-meaning man and several years later his daughter was to become the very first policewoman in Norwich. Whether the police asked him to see Watt, knowing that Watt had previously poured out his matrimonial troubles to him, with a view to learning where the revolver had been deposited, or whether he volunteered his services aiming only to comfort a distraught man, is not known. Perhaps something of both applied.

Constable Walter Slater gave evidence of finding the revolver in night soil at the bottom of a garden situated next to a field, just 200 yards from

Figure 7.4. Magdalen Street in the 1890s where a murderer was harried by a crowd and eventually arrested. Norfolk County Council Library & Information Service

Figure 7.5. The County Police Station at Castle Meadow, sanctuary for the murderer. Barrett & Coe

the scene of the shooting. At this point Watt declared, 'That was found with the aid of Mr Clarke, sir.'

Inspector Flint gave similar evidence of finding the weapon (it is a certainty the Constable had the distasteful task of physical retrieval) and Watt said, 'I thought Mr Clarke found the revolver.'

The Inspector replied, 'I don't say that he didn't. There were at least five persons present.'

Watt: 'It was a statement I made to Mr Clarke that caused the revolver to be found?'

Inspector: 'It was.'

The Chairman asked Watt if he wanted that fact recorded and he said he did.

John Emms, a gunsmith of Orford Hill, gave evidence of examining the recovered weapon and finding it 'similar' to one he sold for eight shillings on 4 April to a man 'very much like the prisoner'. He said the man brought it back on 9 April and he saw that it had been fired and had jammed. It took him three hours to repair it and when he handed it back to the customer it contained five live cartridges and the hammer was down on an empty chamber.

At committal Watt said he wished to put in a statement. He handed it to the Clerk of the Court and although cautioned that anything he said or wrote could be used against him, he insisted it be read openly in Court.

Watt's statement was lengthy, most of it relating to how he had acquired the revolver. He claimed a 'young gentleman' had asked him to purchase a 'pistol' for 'bottle practice', the 'young gentleman' being too young to make the purchase himself. That Watt had received the money, made the purchase, handed over the revolver, met the 'young gentleman' again by chance and taken the weapon back for repair and failed to see the 'young gentleman' again, was described in great detail. The final part of his statement relates to the murder and is worthy of exactness. It is repeated below.

I carried the revolver about with me in my trousers pocket. On Thursday, the 14th, I went to Sprowston to my wife's house to see the children. This was about 2.30 pm. I saw my wife out at the back. I said to her, "Can I see the children, Sophia?" She said, "You don't want to see any children." I said, "I do dear, and I should like to be with them." I handed to her a note which I had written, saying "Read this, dear; you will find this contains the truth." She read it and said, "It's a good job. I told you I should do for you some day or other. If I wanted to take you back I dare not as Jim would not allow me. Beside I have a man I expect coming in my front door every minute who I call my husband and he will soon put you going, so you had better be off." I said to her, "Good God, Sophia, what do you mean?" She said, "I have the law on my side. I can have who I like and go where I like. You are too late now." I then went mad. Having a revolver in my pocket I lost all control and shot at her. I then went to a closet and sat there for some minutes, when I realised my rash act. I walked to the city broken hearted and was shortly after arrested. I solemnly swear I did not go for the purpose of taking away her life – it was her statement that drove me to commit the rash act. George Watt.

The punctuation is odd and while revision could change the tone of the statement its substance remains the same, flying in the face of the evidence of witnesses to the murder and Watt's flight from the scene.

Watt asked that John Clarke be called as a witness and this was done. Watt asked several questions to show that he had frequently been to Clarke's home seeking advice concerning his marriage. Clarke agreed with him. Watt then said that he would like Clarke to have the care of his two young children.

Watt was duly committed to the Assize for trial and on 23 June he appeared before Mr Justice Hawkins, a Judge of strong opinion, acerbic wit and no inclination to like Norwich. At a previous Assize he had started proceedings by castigating the accommodation provided for him by the city, declaring he could not offer the Magistrates his gratitude for their endeavours to provide for the comfort of Her Majesty's Judges, unless they thought he and his marshall had 'the habits and tastes of a Polar bear and an Arctic fox' and Eaton Hall (where he was accommodated) was well fitted for both.

When Watt was asked for his plea he replied, 'I am guilty of murder but not guilty of wilful murder.' Today's lawyers might have difficulty with 'wilful murder', considering 'wilful' to be an unnecessary adjunct. The Court rightly decided that Watt was pleading 'Not Guilty' to murder, hoping for a manslaughter verdict.

Mr E Wild appeared for the defence and he disputed the evidence of Phoebe Paston and Sergeant Martins that Watt had said to his wife 'I shall kill you'. He cross examined Mrs Paston to highlight differences between her present evidence and her deposition. Eventually the upset woman refused to answer any more questions. Wild followed the same line with Sergeant Martins who said he had written Watt's words in his pocket book, which he didn't have with him. This upset the Judge and he gave the Sergeant a torrid time in the witness box before ordering him to go and get his pocket book.

Eliza Chamberlain's query to Watt after the murder and his damning reply, 'What I intended doing for months past', could not be left undisputed. Mr Wild asked Mrs Chamberlain if Watt had been sober at the time. She said he was 'in drink but not drunk'.

Mr Wild: 'Had he been drinking heavily?'

Mrs Chamberlain: 'I cannot say. I was not there when he was drinking.'

The barrister recovered from this brilliant answer to get the witness to speak of her opinion based on experience: she thought Watt had not been drinking heavily. She was unswerving in her recollection of the words used by Watt.

Mr Wild cross examined James Watt to hopefully show that James and his mother had conspired to exaggerate George Watt's bad behaviour as a husband and father.

He asked, 'Is it not a fact that these troubles occurred when he was in drink?'

James Watt replied, 'No, he was just as bad when he was sober.'

Mr Wild: 'He used to drink a great deal?'

James Watt: 'Yes.'

Mr Wild: 'All the fault was always on his side?'

James Watt: 'Yes.'

Mr Wild: 'No provocation by your poor mother, never, all the fault on one side?'

James Watt: 'Yes.'

Mr Wild: 'Always?'

James Watt: 'Yes.'

At the conclusion of his evidence James Watt said, 'Ever since I can remember anything the home has been an unhappy one.'

The prosecutor, Mr Poyser, summed up a succession of telling points in the evidence and sought to remove any sympathy for the prisoner. He said, 'Prisoner had had this revolver in his possession from April 4th to April 14th, and if he had been in this starving condition and had no food, he might have pawned or have sold the weapon and so relieved himself.' Mr Poyser drew the jury's attention to the prisoner's damning statement to Eliza Chamberlain shortly after the murder, when he said he had done what he had intended to do.

Mr Wild in his closing speech admitted that many facts could not be contradicted and it was impossible to deny that the prisoner had killed his wife, or that he had been a bad husband. He spoke of the possible immoral behaviour of Sophia Watt and quoted a legal precedent to show that words of provocation could reduce murder to manslaughter but the Judge promptly overruled that precedent, much to Mr Wild's dismay and thinly disguised irritation.

Mr Wild to the Judge: 'If your Lordship says I have no defence in law I will not be so disrespectful as to address the jury.'

His Lordship: 'This charge of infidelity against this woman is pure invention. A man cannot invent a story of immorality on the part of a woman for the purpose of shielding himself from the consequences of a clearly unlawful act.'

Mr Wild finished defiantly by telling the jury that if they believed the prisoner was expecting another man to call on his wife they should be lenient and find him guilty of manslaughter.

The Judge summed up and dealt a final blow to Mr Wild's plea to the jury. He said, 'Not a breath of suspicion could be cast upon the character of this poor woman.' He cast considerable doubt upon the prisoner's explanation of how he acquired the revolver.

The jury were not long in returning their 'Guilty' verdict.

The Judge, addressing George Watt, said, 'I cannot help the thought crossing my mind that if she had taken you back, the poor woman might have died by the same hand by which she met her death on this sad 14th of April.' He told Watt his 'days were numbered', an ironical reflection upon Watt's declaration to his wife – 'your days are my days', and said 'I see no shade of mitigation for your cruelty'. He duly sentenced him to death.

Watt showed no emotion and, looking briefly up to the public gallery, stepped firmly from the dock.

It is doubtful if anybody expected clemency. George Watt had no illusions. He spoke of his readiness to die saying that with his wife gone he had nothing to live for. His last day was fixed - 12 July at Norwich Prison, the first ever execution at a prison a little over eleven years old.

John Clarke visited Watt the day before the execution and found him in excellent health and sporting a beard. The surge to fitness, fine health and increased weight in a doomed man was similarly commented upon in the case of George Harmer, executed at Norwich Castle in 1886, attributed to the change from austere living – albeit the living would not last.

Watt thanked Clarke for his friendship and asked that his thanks be passed to his solicitors and barrister 'for all they had done'. He asked Clarke to keep an eye on his children and said, 'I shall approach the gallows like a man.' Shaking hands with Clarke he said, 'God bless you; I wish you all success in life.'

John Clarke later spoke of Watt's hard upbringing and said, 'One cannot expect a lot from such a man, and whatever his crime he has not a lot to thank society for.'

The day of the execution came as a beautiful summer's morning. Policemen ringed the walls of the prison and kept a guarded eye on small groups of curious onlookers. At a quarter to nine the prison bell began tolling.

Watt left the condemned cell just before nine o'clock, pinioned by the father and son executioners James and Thomas Billington, a warder holding him each side, the procession of Chaplain, Governor, Surgeon, Under Sheriff and Chief Warder forming around him, walking quickly and firmly along the corridor, turning left and then abruptly right to the scaffold, a permanent structure erected in the coach house. The senior Billington guided Watt onto the trapdoor and placed the white cap over his head and the rope around his neck, the Chaplain chanting, 'Good Lord deliver us' as the younger Billington pulled the lever. George Watt disappeared from view to complete a family tragedy.

Outside the prison there was a flurry of activity as Constables ran to aid Constable Peacock who had been standing by the wall nearest the execution and fainted as the trapdoor clattered. He quickly recovered. A small black flag crept up the prison flagstaff and an official emerged from the gate to post a formal notice that the sentence of death had been carried out. Some of the dwindling spectators stopped to read the notice.

The body was left hanging for the customary hour before being lowered and subjected to a formal inquest, the jury viewing the body, hearing medical evidence of cause of death and returning their automatic verdict of judicial death. George Watt was buried in the south-west corner of the prison grounds where he lies to this day.

There was a final revelation, and not privileged as some theological students would expect. Like many condemned men before him George Watt had spent considerable time with the Prison Chaplain, the Reverend Cox, and had confessed to him that he had indeed purchased the revolver, and with a view to murdering his wife. Nobody had doubted it.

CHAPTER 8

Love and Death:
First of a Trilogy
The Murder of Jane 'Jennie'
Plunkett
1882

ffairs of the heart that conclude in homicide bring sensation, grief and the eternal question: why? Why has love brought death? Three cases many years apart are linked by youth, love and the brutal deaths of young women, each time the murderer professing his love. Individual in their circumstances, alike in their endings, these cases defy comprehension. The murder of Jane Plunkett in 1882 is the less well known of this tragic trilogy, yet it was a cold blooded killing committed against a desperately sad background. It shocked at the time and will surely shock in its retelling.

At the time of her death Jane (known as 'Jennie') Plunkett was twenty-three years of age, a respectable and pleasant young lady seeking to earn her living and in due course settle into married life. Respectability and marriage meant everything in Victorian England. She came from a poor family living in humble surroundings in the village of Felthorpe a few miles outside Norwich and was the eldest of five children. In 1881 she lived and worked as a maidservant at the *Star Hotel* in the Haymarket in Norwich and it was there that she formed a close relationship with the hotel's 'boots' and billiard marker, nineteen-year-old William Abigail.

Abigail was a smartly dressed young man, short in height – not much over five feet, dapper and boyish in appearance with, apparently, an unhappy past. His parents were dead and although born in Great Yarmouth he had lived most of his young life in Norwich, lodging with his grandmother before moving into the *Star Hotel*. His personal history reputedly included an attempt at suicide but 1881 seemed to be his year of promise. He was in regular employment, which gave him decent living accommodation, and had a steady girl friend of whom he was genuinely fond, or so it seemed. But hard times were never far away for so many living in this era, as this young couple were soon to discover.

In the latter part of 1881 a change of management at the *Star Hotel* cost the couple their jobs, and accommodation. William Abigail took up lodgings with his half-brother John Shepherd and wife Eliza at Mill Hill (now Millers Lane) in Norwich, while Jennie went to her family home at Felthorpe. Her affection for William remained unshaken, demonstrated by the letter she wrote on 8 November, 1881. It is replicated in full.

MY DARLING WILLIE – Many thanks for the loving letter I received from you this morning. So glad you arrived home safe, darling. I am longing for Saturday to come. I think I shall not find the time so long this week as I have got plenty of sewing to do. I hope I shall succeed in getting a situation on Saturday, for I dread going before so many of them – it quite upsets me when I think about it. I hope the next lady will have a pleasant look. Sorry you did not see anything in the paper that would suit either of us. I shall be thankful when you get settled and working for a home for us darling. You say I must make myself happy, but I cannot and never shall be time I am away from you, for you are my heart's desire. I am so glad darling that we can be together once a week. I really do not know whatever I should do if I could not see you at all. I could not stop here now, darling. I will bring these few lines to a close, hoping they will meet you well and happy, darling. With fondest love and lots of kisses when we meet from your loving JENNIE

Their fortunes improved. William obtained a job as a waiter at the Albert Café in Prince of Wales Road and Jennie went into the service of Mr and Mrs Burlingham at Mousehold. Then their fortunes took a turn for the worse. Jennie became pregnant. Her condition not only threatened her employment, it promised social stigma. They resolved this personal crisis by telling people they had married by special licence and Jennie showed a wedding ring on her finger.

No record was ever found of the couple's marriage, and the police looked, but as far as Jennie and William were concerned they were man and wife. The letter written by Jennie on 5 April 1882 from Mousehold, replicated below, amply demonstrates her thinking.

MY VERY DEAREST HUSBAND – I was so pleased to hear from you this morning and that you are well. I feel in better spirits since I received your letter and, darling, I wish you not to worry [hurry?] down here tomorrow night (Thursday). I shall be out to tea with you, dear husband, on Friday, but cannot say what time I shall see you. I do not expect I shall be out in the morning, so, darling, I wish you to rest yourself in bed as long as you can; and I think it would be best for me to come down to Eliza by myself, as I do not know what time I shall get out, it may be late and it may be soon. Of course I shall try my best to get away as soon as I can, so I shall expect to find you there, darling husband. I am so anxious to see you and know all particulars. My darling husband I must come to a close, expecting to see you on Friday, with fondest love and lots of kisses when we meet. From your ever affectionate wife. J.A.

In April Jennie's pregnancy was well advanced and she inevitably lost her job. On Friday, 21 April, William Abigail asked Eliza Shepherd to speak to her husband about Jennie lodging at Mill Hill for a few days. He said it would only be until Tuesday when she would be moving in with a friend, and by the end of the week he would have a new home ready for her. Jennie would later tell a slightly different story: that she was moving in with 'her people' on the Tuesday. The Shepherds believed William and Jennie were married.

John Shepherd agreed to Abigail's request and Jennie arrived with her effects on the Saturday evening, bringing some disruption to the normal sleeping arrangements. Mrs Shepherd's brother, George Peachman, eight years old and described by everybody as a 'little lad', had to give up the upstairs bedroom he shared with Abigail, moving downstairs to sleep on a formation of chairs near the back door, possibly uncomfortable but to prove strategically and evidentially important. Mr and Mrs Shepherd slept next to the room given to the 'married' couple but, significantly, Mrs Shepherd was hard of hearing and her husband was a lamplighter who consequently had to leave the house at an exceptionally early hour.

The Shepherds observed that the young couple appeared happy and comfortable on the Sunday and the Monday, George treating his young lady with affection and tenderness, calling her 'my dear' and 'darling'. On the Monday evening the young couple went out together seemingly without a care in the world, yet William Abigail's mind must have been in turmoil. For reasons known only to him he had given up his job at the café and on this Monday evening he was a young man with no job, no money and heavy responsibilities, which included finding accommodation for his pregnant 'wife'. It is most unlikely that arrangements existed for her to move on Tuesday; and the provision of a new home on the Saturday, as he had informed the Shepherds, was patently untrue. Inexplicably he did possess something of value: a firearm.

On the Sunday evening Abigail saw John Shepherd in the kitchen at Mill Hill and asked, 'Would you like to have something to blow birds' guts out with?'

Shepherd replied simply, 'Yes', and Abigail produced a fully loaded revolver. The two men went for a walk and Shepherd fired four shots at birds and Abigail then fired two shots. They returned to Mill Hill and Abigail produced a box of cartridges saying he had bought a box of fifty for 2s 6d. Where and why he had acquired the weapon and ammunition did not enter the conversation, according to Shepherd, although it might seem natural to have put these questions.

On Monday night Mr and Mrs Shepherd retired early, the regular practice of a lamplighter and wife, and the 'little lad', George Peachman, made himself as comfortable as possible in the downstairs back room.

John Shepherd rose at his normal early hour and went to work, returning at half-past four and at twenty minutes to five shouting the time up the stairs to William Abigail, a regular early call that was now, unknowing to Shepherd, obsolete. Abigail called back 'All right' but remained in the bedroom. He could not leave the house without passing very close to the sleeping George Peachman.

John Shepherd left the house to work in his garden, remaining there until seven o'clock and hearing nothing unusual. His wife rarely heard anything unusual because of her defective hearing.

At around half-past six George Peachman jerked awake to a loud 'bang', followed immediately by another. Young he may have been but he had no doubt he had heard gunshots. He froze, waiting for a third shot, which did not come. The frightened lad went to the bottom of the stairs and called loudly and eventually penetrated Mrs Shepherd's hearing.

'There's a gun gone off,' exclaimed the frightened boy.

'There's nothing to be afraid of,' reassured Mrs Shepherd, ushering the boy back to his sleeping position.

Ten to fifteen minutes after being reassured the boy became alert again, picking up on booted footsteps coming down the stairs. The footsteps left by the back door, the owner unseen but just a door's width away from the apprehensive listener. The back door closed, the footsteps faded and a pondering boy had no more sleep.

At seven o'clock John Shepherd returned from the garden and Mrs Shepherd rose to begin another day, gratefully joined by her little brother.

Mrs Shepherd went into William and Jennie's bedroom at eight o'clock and saw Jennie in bed, lying on her side with the bedclothes up to her ears, one arm trailing outside the bed. William was not there, and she would not have expected him to be. A dented pillow indicated that he had been present.

Taking hold of Jennie's arm and finding it cold to the touch, and noticing blood on the pillow, Mrs Shepherd ran from the room, rousing and crying to her husband, 'Jennie has killed herself'.

John Shepherd looked at Jennie, seeing blood dripping from her exposed hand and oozing from her neck, her slightly exposed face darkening to a blue shade. Without disturbing the body he left the house and ran to the police station. He returned with Constable Edmund Woollard.

Constable Woollard recorded the time he accompanied John Shepherd to the house as 8.20 am. He noted that the body was lying face down, on its right side, the head resting on an outstretched right arm, the left arm hanging from the bed. He found the pillow and bed saturated with blood and noted a wound behind the left ear, a 'black spot' on a sheet corresponding to a 'black spot' on the pillow, both spots smelling of

Figure 8.1. A tragedy revealed. David Rowlands

gunpowder, and further black spots on the left shoulder of her nightdress near her left breast with a small hole in the nightdress. He turned the bedclothes down and discovered a six-chambered revolver lying near the knees of the body, the muzzle pointing downwards. Four chambers were loaded. An impression in the bed showed that another person had lain alongside her.

Doctor Robert Mills, the Police Surgeon, arrived and recorded two wounds, one in the neck two inches below the root of the left ear stained with gunpowder and singeing the surrounding hair, and one in the side of the body below the left breast. His post-mortem examination retrieved two bullets, one that had entered the neck, travelled upward and distorted and splintered in the temple, splinters entering the brain, and one that had entered the side between the fourth and fifth ribs and penetrated the heart. He diagnosed that both wounds were fatal, the neck and head wound perhaps not instantaneous but the heart wound certainly so. He thought that the neck wound had been the first wound received and could not possibly have been inflicted by the deceased. The side wound could physically have come from the deceased, but not after receiving the head wound. He thought her arm had been lifted to fire the second shot into her body. Noting the position she was lying in and the peaceful expression on her face he deduced she been killed in her sleep, unaware of how and by whose hand she had died. In his opinion Jennie was eight months pregnant. Two persons had died in that bedroom.

Detective Inspector Robert Mason went to the house, viewed the body and made enquiries of those present, leaving with John Shepherd in a hansom cab in what may be seen in the sinister and timeless terminology of a man assisting the police with their enquiries, in this case genuinely so. Mason needed Shepherd to identify Abigail. They sped to the Albert Café only to find that Abigail was no longer employed there. The cab moved on to the Guildhall Police Station, meeting the Chief Constable, Robert Hitchman, outside. Three men stood on the pavement outside the Guildhall, Inspector Mason reporting to his Chief Constable and Shepherd describing Abigail, a fourth man, a lurking newspaper reporter, edging closer.

Shepherd stopped in mid-description of Abigail, staring and blurting out, 'There he is!'

Abigail walked from Dove Street into Guildhall Hill but where he was going to or coming from, and why he was so close to the police station after committing murder was never known. Factually, he was seized and hustled into the police station.

Inspector Mason told Abigail he was arresting him for murdering his 'wife' with a revolver and Abigail replied, without any sign of surprise, 'Is she dead?'

Inspector Mason said, 'Yes, I have just seen the body.' He searched his prisoner and drew the remark, 'You'll find no weapons on me.'

An examination of Abigail's clothing found patches of blood on the left sleeve of his shirt. If he sought to explain or was asked to explain the stains it went unrecorded. He did make a verbal statement that revealed his thinking, or lack of it. He asked where the police had been looking for him and continued, 'How do you know I murdered my wife? Nobody saw me do it. She had her arms and could use them as well as me.'

Abigail had one halfpenny upon him, truly a man in desperate straits.

William Abigail was charged with the murder of Jane Plunkett and committal proceedings began the next day, the inquest a day later at *The Whalebone* public house. The inquest had no problems in returning a verdict of murder by Abigail.

The committal attracted a large crowd and was notable for Abigail's attitude in the courtroom. He adopted an air of indifference that some

Figure 8.2. THERE HE IS! The Chief Constable and Detective Inspector stood outside the Guildhall, left, listening to a witness describing the murder suspect, interrupted by the suspect suddenly appearing from Dove Street, right. Norfolk County Council Library & Information Service

saw as studied insolence, folding his arms, impassive to the exhibited grief of Jennie's parents. Her father had to be helped from the courtroom and her mother, giving evidence of identifying her daughter's body, was equally distressed. Abigail remained unmoved.

The committal went down the same path of evidence as the inquest, consternation taking over when the exhibited revolver was found to be still loaded. The police were ordered to remove and unload the weapon following which the committal adjourned to allow more enquiries, principally to find the origin of the revolver and verify the blood on Abigail's clothing. At the resumed committal Abigail was brought early from Norwich Castle, frustrating a large crowd that later gathered outside the Guildhall.

In 1882 evidence of blood typing was some way off and when the blood on Abigail was found to be human it was circumstantially presumed that it belonged to Jane Plunkett. Evidence matching the revolver with the intact bullet extracted from the body had similar limitations. A gunsmith gave evidence that the revolver was of a common make, of German origin, and the intact bullet from the body fitted it. That it would have fitted other guns was something for the defence to postulate, if they chose. The next century would leave no doubt on matching blood samples and guns with bullets.

On 29 April 1882 Abigail was committed to stand trial at the Assize. He reserved his defence. On 30 April the woman who loved him and carried his child was buried in the grounds of Felthorpe Parish Church. Funeral costs were met by a subscription organised by the Chief Constable and Norwich City Police, and her tombstone was personally contributed by the Chief Constable. There were tremendous scenes of grief at the graveside from Jennie's parents, brothers and sisters, and many who had known her. The press reported a public feeling of tenderness to the young lady and outspoken bitterness to her killer.

Abigail did not have to wait long for his trial. It took place at the Norfolk and Suffolk Assize at Ipswich on 6 May before Baron Pollock. It is likely that a venue away from Norwich, where feelings were running high against Abigail, was deemed expedient. He pleaded 'Not Guilty' and again displayed an attitude that infuriated the press. The *Eastern Evening News* reported that he 'manifested the same callousness' that attended his previous appearances and 'characterised him when first taken into custody'.

The Judge instructed Mr Poyser to defend the prisoner and Mr Blofeld appeared for the prosecution. Mr Blofeld's task, as straightforward as it

Figure 8.3. Chief Constable Robert Hitchman, joint arresting officer and funeral benefactor. Hitchman was the first and longest serving Chief Constable of Norwich, from 1859 to 1897.
Police Archive

seemed, lacked the support of a clear-cut motive. He offered a motive. In his view the prisoner was desperate and despairing. He had no money, no job, no proper home and a 'wife' and imminently a child to support. Perhaps, proposed Mr Blofeld, the prisoner had sought to remove himself of all his responsibilities. He submitted that medical evidence overwhelmingly disproved any submission that Jane Plunkett killed herself.

Mr Poyser thought otherwise and described various contortions that, in his view, could have related to what he called 'self-murder' and would have provided the scene found by the Shepherds. He addressed the jury in emotional terms, referring to the 'few things' gathered by the prisoner in anticipation of his new home and the affection he had always shown to the young woman he loved. He asked if she could not have killed herself in a moment of despair, 'knowing the trouble about to come upon her'. This heart-rending defence speech to the jury, probably delivered with the saddened expression peculiar to lawyers, wrought a change in Abigail. He broke down in the dock, weeping bitterly.

Figure 8.4. Jane Plunkett's headstone reads: 'This stone was erected by the Chief Constable of Norwich in memory of Jane Plunkett aged 23 years who was murdered in Norwich on the 25th April 1882'. The author

The Judge said the evidence was circumstantial but in the circumstances it could not be anything else. He said it was impossible to present a motive to the jury and it would be dangerous to consider one presented by one side or the other. He reviewed the evidence as presented and the jury retired, returning after fifteen minutes.

The foreman declared their verdict: 'Guilty'. He added a rider – a strong recommendation for mercy on account of the youth of the prisoner.

The Judge told Abigail he would take care the recommendation for mercy was forwarded to the proper authorities, sternly adding, 'You will not allow it in any way to lead you to indulge in the hope that the sentence I am about to pass will not be carried out according to law.' In time honoured form he passed sentence of death, during which Abigail continued to weep.

The jury's recommendation, and a well-signed petition, failed to persuade the Home Secretary. William Abigail, a teenager, was scheduled to die on Monday, 22 May 1882, completing a fast-track implementation of justice, even for those days. Rules required three Sundays to elapse between sentence and execution and this immature youth was to see those three

Sundays, just. He would be put to death less than a month after committing murder. Two lovers and an unborn dying within one month from a moment of madness!

Did the jury's recommendation of mercy fail upon Abigail's attitude, seen again at the trial until the moment he broke down? Repentance and a plea from the heart of this immature youth might have saved his life. His cold and indifferent attitude returned after the trial. Mr and Mrs Shepherd visited him at Norwich Castle and when Mrs Shepherd burst into tears he asked, 'What have you to cry for?' When she said she was sorry for him he told her to cheer up, adding, 'The disgrace upon you will pass off like dew before the sunshine.'

John Shepherd didn't feel so sorry for his half-brother. He said that he hoped Abigail would reflect upon what he had done whereupon Abigail retorted, 'That has nothing to do with you', threatening to terminate the interview. When his grandmother visited him he did terminate the interview.

Abigail slept and ate well, maintained his stolid indifference and refused to confess the crime. But on the morning of Sunday, 21 May, twenty-four hours before he was due to die, he attended the prison chapel service and while singing the hymn 'I am not worthy, Holy Lord' he broke down. The Chaplain's sermon on the subject of 'thou shalt not kill' caused more distress and that same evening he saw the Chaplain and confessed to murdering Jane. That confession was forwarded to the Home Office but never publicised and, apparently, never archived.

The Monday morning came dry, warm and sunny. Eight o'clock was fixed as the time William Abigail would leave this world. The executioner, William Marwood, entered the castle via the Shirehall, accompanied by the usual retinue of officials and press. At quarter to eight the bell of St Peter Mancroft began tolling. Two minutes before eight o'clock the melancholy procession appeared at the entrance to the tiny yard, measuring only 'sixteen paces by five paces', on the Castle Meadow side opposite Opie Street, entering from the bath-house and moving in what the press described as 'a slow and measured tread', halting as Marwoood moved forward and strapped a belt around Abigail's waist, next swiftly pinioning his arms to the belt and motioning the procession to continue towards the strongly built, starkly black gallows. The press reported that Abigail looked 'pale and haggard as if he had spent the night with tears', walking unsteadily to the gallows gently urged by Marwood.

The Chaplain recited from the *Book of Common Prayer* and the doomed man fervently repeated the words, his hands clasped, his face turned upwards. Marwood guided him over the trapdoor, dropped the white cap over his head and adjusted the rope. Abigail called, 'Lord Jesus receive my spirit,' dropping from sight as Marwood pulled the lever, falling nine feet and, according to the attentive press, 'rebounding against the padded sides of the pit'; like his lover he died instantly. But he knew why and how! A signal was given to a warder on the ramparts and he hoisted the black flag above the castle. People assembled at the Castle Gate stared at the fluttering flag before quietly walking away.

The inquest in the castle at ten o'clock was the usual formality. The jury viewed the body laid in a black coffin, the Castle Governor gave evidence of identity and lawful sentence, and the Prison Surgeon gave evidence of death. William George Abigail was buried in the precincts of Norwich Castle, the final act in a chapter of tragic acts.

CHAPTER 9

Love and Death:
Second of a Trilogy
The Murder of Eleanor
'Nellie' Howard
1908

The young man stumbled into the public house with mud on his coat, shaking and dripping blood. He ordered a half pint of ale; drank some, spilt a lot. He ordered another, swearing as he did so, claiming he had fallen from his bicycle. An alarmed landlady refused to serve him and told him to 'clear off'. He left, leaving blood on the floor. Later that night the police brought his girl friend to the public house on a cart. They laid her lifeless and disfigured body in the coach house.

At first light on Friday, 30 October 1908, the police had a clearer view of the body in the coach house of *The Maid's Head Inn* at Catton. The young woman had been attractive, now she was frozen in death with glaring face and shoulder wounds, her clothing heavily bloodstained. Policemen studied what had once been beautiful. She was of medium height, prettily dressed in a dark green skirt and bodice with dainty white gloves, all bloodied, wearing black stockings and a hat of chipped straw decorated with artificial flowers. Her delicate complexion, now marred by a vivid wound, was topped by black eyebrows and a mass of black hair gathered loosely over her forehead. She appeared to have dressed in her best finery. All who saw her were moved by the tragedy that lay before them. Comment was made upon the touching sight of a little bunch of flowers pinned to her left breast. Those who commented were not to know that she had not placed that buttonhole picture there.

Her wounds were vicious. In the neck and shoulder a gaping puncture wound was large enough to admit a finger up to the knuckle, and her face had been slashed downwards and across the right cheek to the corner of the mouth. Blood had spilled from these wounds down her clothes, still oozing as she lay in the coach house. Her pockets revealed a handkerchief, small key, packet of chocolates and a purse containing a shilling and two coppers. She lay on a wooden cart, beautiful and distorted, and anonymous. The *Eastern Daily Press* of that morning described her as a 'painful and horrifying sight'.

A young woman dressed in her best, looking her best, meant the company of a male friend, the police thought. She had probably known her killer, pleading with him, hurting and dying in terror and without comprehension. Her early identification would be everything to the investigation. So it proved. The power of spreading bad news soon offered an identity, to be confirmed at nine twenty-five that morning by the man who had killed her.

Eleanor Elizabeth Howard, sometimes called Ellen, more frequently Nellie, was nineteen years of age and lived with her grandparents at Radford Hall Farm at Hainford where they were in service. The eldest of six children she had lived with her grandparents since childhood, a seemingly unforced and acceptable arrangement to all concerned. Her mother had been employed as a cook at Hainford Hall.

Nellie, as we shall call her – as she called herself, had been in service in Norwich until eight months before her death. Described as 'a good, steady girl' she had been courting a young Norwich man named Horace Larter for just over two years, but in the past few months, possibly influenced by her grandparents, they had been seeing less of each other. Nellie had told her grandfather that Larter had threatened to shoot her if she went with anyone else.

Horace Larter was also nineteen years of age, presentable but rough in his manner, given to swearing and drinking. He lived with his parents at Ber Street Gates in the city and worked in his father's business as a fish dealer, keeping a shellfish stall outside the Agricultural Hall at Bank Plain.

Nellie died on the evening of Thursday, 29 October 1908, and the preceding events of that day, morning and afternoon, were an acceleration and culmination of her boyfriend's festering thoughts, his bitterness at a waning relationship. Her death was no spur of the moment, unplanned, unforeseen tragedy. Horace Larter had made his mind up. On the morning of that day he told George Howard (co-incidental name), a cabman on the rank opposite the Agricultural Hall, that he was having a day off to see his sweetheart and he got the cabman to look after his stall while he went into

London Street to buy a box of chocolates. He also went to the cutler's shop of Pearsons in Bedford Street where he purchased a heavy spear-pointed clasp knife.

Nellie had that morning received a letter from Larter inviting her to meet him in Norwich, little knowing its dreadful implication. A portion found by the police reads:

> So if we are to part we can part the very best of friends so do come up, and we can go to the exhibition together. Hope to meet you at two o'clock as I shall come to meet you. So do come up if for the last time. Glad you like my chocolates. So do come up to Norwich for the sake of the time we have had. Hope you have time to write. My mother would like to see you Thursday, as father is out, and with my affectionate love to you, I remain, Horace.
>
> I shall come if you have not time to write, so I shall meet you coming along. Start at two.

Letters from Nellie to Larter were found in his bedroom, the last, dated 19 October, reads:

> My Dear Horace, Just a few lines to let you know that I arrived home safe last Wednesday night. Hoping these few lines will find you well as I am not going out to service just yet, but I may come up to see you for the day, that is, if you wish me too. You promised me you would send me that ring but you have not fulfilled your promise yet. Dear Horace, I should very much like to have some chocolate, as I have not had any off you lately. It will be a treat for you to send me some. Mabel sends her best respects to you. Give my love to your mother. I now close with fondest love to you – I remain, your loving sweetheart,
>
> Nellie

This letter hardly points to a disrupted love affair and imminent separation, yet that is how Larter saw their association.

Early in the afternoon of her last day Nellie bid her grandfather goodbye and set off walking to Norwich. At two forty-five Larter boarded a tram in Magdalen Street and drew attention when he threw a 'stick' he was carrying at the side of the tram, following which he went to the footboard in an excited state. The conductor asked him to stand inside the tram and he obliged, saying, 'Oh dear! I've been on the juice for three days.'

The conductor, William Knyvett, knew Larter and said, 'What, is the mussel trade looking up?'

Larter replied, 'My trade is like yours. Old women come and spend one-and-a-halfpence and want a clean towel, and think they've bought the —————— show.' He then said, 'I had six bottles of cider last night and whisky.'

Knyvett asked, 'What is the meaning of you going on the drink like this?'

Larter thought before replying, 'I have got wrong with my missus. I will put an end to this today.'

As the tram approached *The Whalebone* public house at the bottom of St Clement's Hill, Larter suddenly said, 'I'm going to have a drink before I go any further; you can't get away to come and have one?'

Knyvett declined to leave his tram and watched Larter enter the public house. If Larter planned to commit murder he had no thought of keeping a low profile, or did he care?

The landlord of *The Whalebone*, William Wright, remembered Larter coming in briefly at about three o'clock, and again at about half-past three when he had a young lady with him. She drank lemonade and he had whisky.

At 5.30 pm Larter walked with Nellie to the cab rank at the Agricultural Hall and asked George Howard to drive them to Ber Street Gates. Howard obliged and on the way they stopped at *The Norwich Arms* for refreshment. Nellie remained in the cab while Larter and the cabman went inside. Larter took a glass of port wine out to her. They continued to Larter's home where Larter and Nellie went inside, the cab waiting five minutes for their return. Back at the Agricultural Hall Larter tried to persuade Howard to drive them to *The Maid's Head* at Catton. Howard refused, saying he had other orders, though he may have been influenced by Larter not paying him for the service he had already rendered.

Larter and Nellie boarded a tram near the Agricultural Hall and once again the conductor knew Larter. George Chaplin recalled that Larter had obviously been drinking and when the couple got off his tram at *The Whalebone* public house, at about six o'clock, Larter insisted on shaking his hand, telling him he was about to walk to Hainford, creating another in a trail of potential witnesses. If he was really planning a murder he was not planning to get away with it. Chaplin watched the couple walk into St Clement's Hill and stop at a sweet shop. Nellie's love of chocolate had interrupted their journey.

A little over an hour later Larter entered *The Maid's Head Inn* in Spixworth Road (a continuation of St Clement's Hill), excited, bleeding and spilling beer, swearing and getting himself ejected.

Figure 9.1. The victim's last journey began by tram from Bank Plain. The Agricultural Hall is on the right. Norfolk County Council Library & Information Service

Around 7.30 pm he entered *The Whalebone*, still excited, ordering a 'small lemonade'. William Wright served him, noticing and remarking upon the blood on his hands and clothing. Larter said he had had an accident with his bicycle. The sharp-eyed landlord commented upon the heavy clasp knife protruding from Larter's waistcoat pocket, asking if the opened blade had cut him when he fell from the bicycle. Larter did not reply but took the knife from his pocket, seen by the landlord as a 'buck-handled clasp knife with a rather long pointed blade', closed the blade and replaced the knife, in doing so revealing a deep cut to his right forefinger.

Before the inquisitive landlord could pose further questions Larter finished his drink, and said, 'Good night', adding 'Perhaps I shall see you later.' He must have known William Wright was another witness against him.

Horace Larter went on to create yet another witness, one he presented with a confession. After leaving *The Whalebone* he visited his sister, Florence Ludkin, in Sprowston Road, telling her he was 'boozy', which she could see for herself. He asked to see Florence's husband and was tersely informed that he was in bed and was not to be disturbed. He then asked for a cup of tea and Florence said she had none. He said he had cut his hand and asked if he could wash it.

His sister replied, 'No, you will mess the place up, let me do it for you.' She told him to sit still on the chair or he would fall over but instead he walked to the door, saying, 'Will you shake hands with me for the last time? I've killed Nellie.' As he walked away from his thunderstruck sister he said, 'I shall give myself up to the first Constable I come to.'

He did not come upon a Constable and arrived home at around half-past eight, seen by his father and his younger brother with whom he quarrelled before going to bed. On the Spixworth Road, a quarter of a mile from the nearest house, on what was described as 'an exceedingly dark night', Nellie Howard lay on her side in the lee of a roadside hedge, her head on her left arm, blood running through her clothes to the chocolates in her pocket.

At ten minutes to nine Police Sergeant Walter Slater, walking from Catton to Spixworth and probing ahead with his lamp, lit up Nellie's body. Closer examination revealed the full horror of his find and, taking into consideration the recentness of the injuries and the isolation of the spot, he darted into the adjoining field, spraying his lamp over wheat sheaves for a hiding murderer. But Horace Larter had by now reached his home.

Sergeant Slater made for the nearest habitation, the blacksmith's shop of Joseph Laws, and sent Laws to the city to obtain a doctor and inform the County Police Station.

Doctor Flack set out from Magdalen Road on his bicycle but lost his way and did not arrive until ten minutes to eleven, and then only by following an *Eastern Daily Press* reporter. Constable Sizeland arrived earlier, followed by Inspector Roy.

The doctor examined the body by lamplight under the intent gaze of the police, press and blacksmith, confirming what was obvious – the young woman had suffered at least two terrible wounds and was dead, and not too long previously. They placed her on the blacksmith's cart and took her to the coach house at *The Maid's Head Inn*.

At dawn the police searched the road and adjoining area. They found spots of blood 150 yards in the Spixworth direction from the body, but no signs of a struggle. It meant the couple had turned back towards Norwich, Nellie possibly running, possibly wounded. Or had Larter cut himself at that point? Blood grouping was too far away for this 1908 case.

Another spot of blood was found on the roadside between where the body had fallen and Norwich and this can safely be attributed to Larter's cut hand, likewise blood on the floor of *The Maid's Head Inn*.

Figure 9.2. Camera conscious bystanders and police mill around a scene of death. Sergeant Slater dominates the road.

The post-mortem examination revealed a third wound upon Nellie, a knife wound in her back that had just missed her spinal column. Doctor Flack said that the two inches deep puncture wound in her neck and shoulder had severed an artery and been the fatal wound. She had not been sexually mistreated.

Figure 9.3. Two lines of morbid public lead to the spot where 'Nellie' Howard died. Preserving a crime scene was not a consideration in those days, in fact the police took up a collection at the spot to pay for the funeral.

The Friday morning saw the investigation moving quickly to revelation on all fronts. Inspector Roy and Sergeant Slater took Nellie's grandfather to *The Maid's Head* coach house and the grief stricken man identified Nellie. He was taken home where her grandmother collapsed at the confirming news.

At Buxton Police Station, a farmer's assistant named William Arnold handed in a rattee cane and umbrella he had found on the Spixworth Road the previous evening. He pinpointed his find a quarter of a mile the Spixworth side of where he had cycled past two policemen standing over a young woman. Mabel Smithson, Nellie's cousin, also living at Radford Hall Farm, identified the umbrella as belonging to Nellie, taken with her when she went to meet Larter. (William Kynvett, tram conductor, would have recalled the rattee cane). Larter and Nellie had clearly turned back in some disorder.

At nine thirty-five that morning Larter presented himself at the Guildhall Police Station in Norwich and saw Inspector William Ebbage.

Larter said, in the form of a question, 'You want to see me about that job last night?'

Inspector Ebbage didn't particularly want to see Larter and all he knew of the 'job last night' was what he had just read in the morning newspaper headed 'Terrible Murder Near Norwich'. But he noted that Larter was visibly excited and his hand was bound by a handkerchief.

Larter blurted out, 'I was there, and I happened to —', he broke off, and then continued, 'Well, we had a little bit of nonsense. The old woman interfered. Her people, I mean. In a fit of jealousy I suppose. I think that is the case.'

Inspector Ebbage asked 'what job' Larter was referring to, though he now had a good idea, and received the reply, 'The murder charge at Hainford, Catton, last night. I have made a good job of it this time: I thought I would make a good job of it whilst I was about it.'

Larter was taken into custody and searched. Blood was found in large quantities on his jacket and on the front of his trousers, going through to his thigh and knee. Small spots were found on his right boot. When his hand was unbound cuts were found at the base of the second and third fingers and upon the tip of the little finger. There were six fine scratches across the back of his left hand and a half-inch abrasion between the first and second finger with the skin looking as if he had been nipped or bitten out. Nellie had fought for her life.

Inspector Roy and Sergeant Fuller of the county force, by now looking for Larter, were soon at the Guildhall where Larter greeted them with, 'What's done cannot be undone'. Inspector Roy told him he would be charged with murdering Eleanor Howard and Larter replied, 'Yes, that is alright, but it is Nellie Howard, not Eleanor Howard.' He was taken to the County Police Station at Castle Meadow and in his cell that evening he volunteered a written statement to Constable Poulter. This statement requires complete repetition:

> I met her about three o'clock on Elm Hill. I had rather a job to get her to come with me, because I could see she didn't want me. I took her for a cab drive round Norwich, and went to *The Norwich Arms* in Ber Street. I treated her to two glasses of port, and I also treated the cabman. I gave a man threepence to hold the horse time the cabman came inside me. She would not come in the pub herself. I quite intended enjoying myself as I knew she did not want me, and I had made up my mind to kill her. I went down to Pearsons the same morning and bought a clasp knife, which I gave a shilling for. I felt as if I could have murdered anyone if I saw them speaking to her. I loved her so, and this is all through love and jealousy. This is what hate and love will do. I intended her not to make a ———— fool of me. After we had enjoyed ourselves in Norwich, I walked along the road to take her home. It was about six o'clock when we started quarrelling. She told me she did not want me, and I said, "You shall not ———————— have anyone else." That was about 6.30 when I felt like a madman. I caught her by the throat with one hand, and stabbed her twice with the other. Just as she was turning round when I thought to walk away, I stabbed her again, when she fell down and never spoke again. I stood by her quite five minutes, and I thought I would do myself in. Then a change came over me. I knelt down in a pool of blood, which you will see on my trousers, and kissed her when she was dead. I lifted her head to see if she was really dead, and then I pinned a buttonhole on her and left her. Never mind, I suppose her soul is now in heaven. If it was not for her people this never would have happened. They have been saying things about me so I should not have her, and I think it is about the best thing I could have done. I have had this on my mind a long time.

The buttonhole flowers had been poignantly explained: once again the killer of a loved one is moved to a touching farewell, tempered by the callousness of his conclusions. And it is suggested that he has confused St Clement's Hill with Elm Hill.

The inquest and committal by Magistrates for trial were formalities in which Larter was attentive but generally unmoved. The inquest took place at *The Maid's Head Inn* on the Monday under the County Coroner, Mr H Culley. Nellie still reposed in the coach house where she was viewed by the jury. Unusually, Larter appeared at the hearing flanked by two prison warders. During the reading of his statement he fixed his eyes firmly downwards.

His sister Florence broke down as she gave her evidence and when she had finished he called out, 'Goodbye.'

She replied, 'Goodbye Horrie' and tearfully left the room.

The inquest jury returned a verdict of murder against Larter and he called out, 'Thank you gentlemen, one and all.'

The funeral of Nellie Howard took place on 4 November and once again the police sought to defray the cost. A public subscription had been organised by Sergeant Slater, Constable Sizeland and Hainford's own Constable Merry, the latter showing great initiative by collecting from persons wishing to view the scene of Nellie's death. £5 19s was given to Nellie's grandfather.

Figure 9.4. The officer in charge of the case, Inspector Walter Roy, pictured after his promotion to Superintendent. Police Archive

Figure 9.5. The inquest takes place at The Maid's Head Inn.

Nellie had been moved from the coach house to Radford Hall Farm and from there the tearful funeral procession wended its way through country lanes behind the flower covered wheeled bier containing Nellie's coffin. Her mother was too overcome to follow and her father collapsed and was taken home before the procession reached the new church at Hainford. After the service the mourners reassembled and walked a mile behind the trundling bier to Nellie's interment at Hainford's old church, the route lined with country folk paying their last respects, the fading light and swirling leaves of a late autumn afternoon adding to the sombre occasion. Many of those present, including the press, were visibly moved by Nellie's last journey. At the crowded graveside, after a prayer and singing of a hymn, the Vicar expressed the family's thanks to all who had sympathised, speaking of the 'unselfish way in which members of the police force had acted', referring particularly to the kindness of Constable Merry and his action in making a collection of those wishing to 'view the scene of this dreadful deed'.

The committal by Magistrates took place on 7 November with Larter once again calm and composed, spending most of the hearing with his arms folded across his chest. He made one interruption. As Inspector Ebbage gave his evidence Larter leapt up and announced, 'If I had made a good job of it, as I told the policeman I intended, I should not be here now.'

History was made at the committal when Charles Aldous, a photographic artist of White Lion Street, produced photographs showing where Nellie

Figures 9.6 & 9.7. The funeral of 'Nellie' Howard.

died. Photographing a murder scene for evidential purposes was a glimpse into the future, let down in this case by the pictures reappearing for sale as postcards.

The police called additional medical evidence. Doctor Riviere of Bethel Street had examined the cuts and abrasions on Larter's hand, finding the cuts had uneven and lacerated edges. Evidence of a struggle?

Doctor Flack gave evidence of the wounds inflicted upon Nellie but made no comparison with the murder weapon; and Pearson's shop assistant gave evidence of selling the weapon but didn't identify it. Where had the clasp knife, last seen by William Wright, got to? The police seemingly did not have it. Yet they must have asked the freely confessing owner and user what he had done with it. Records and accounts of the inquest and committal are not forthcoming on this point and the case depositions are not in the National Archives. We have to presume the knife was not found, disposed of by Larter after he left *The Whalebone* public house.

Larter was committed to Norwich Prison to await his Assize trial – to be a most extraordinary affair.

The Assize Court was packed on 27 January 1909 when Larter appeared before Mr Justice Lawrence. A crowd of curious sightseers waited outside trying to snatch a glimpse of the prisoner arriving in the prison van.

Mr H Lawless appeared for the prosecution and the Judge requested Mr A Taylor to conduct the prisoner's defence. Neither barrister found himself employed.

Larter stepped briskly into the dock, neatly dressed in a blue suit, and listened intently as the Clerk of the Court read the charge of murder. He was asked for his plea.

'Guilty' called Larter in a loud voice. A mixture of surprise and consternation rippled through the Court. The press reporter noted that Larter was 'coldly indifferent'.

The Judge: 'Do you know what you are pleading guilty to?'

Larter: 'Yes, my Lord.'

Judge: 'Do you know the consequences?'

Larter: 'Yes, my Lord.'

Judge (obviously in an incredulous voice): 'You wish to plead guilty?'

Larter: 'Yes, my Lord.'

Judge: 'There is a learned counsel who is kind enough to say he will defend you. Under those circumstances do you wish to plead guilty? I don't wish to interfere. You know what you are doing?' (The last sentence again pitched to incredulity.)

Larter: 'I beg your pardon.'

The Judge tried again, offering 'learned counsel'.

Larter said he 'would sooner plead guilty'.

The Judge again drew attention to the consequences and got the now standard response of 'Yes, my Lord.'

The Judge wearily nodded to the Clerk of the Court who stood up and addressed Larter. 'You stand convicted on your own confession of the crime of wilful murder. Have you anything to say why judgement of death should not be pronounced on you according to law?'

Larter replied firmly, 'No, my Lord.'

The Courtroom, buzzing with excitement, was called to silence to hear the death sentence. With the black cap upon his head the Judge spoke of the sequence of events on the fateful Thursday, telling Larter 'you made up your mind to take that girl's life', and 'anything more cruel, more hard-hearted, it is hardly possible to conceive'. He sentenced him to death and as he solemnly intoned 'May the Lord have mercy upon your soul' Larter trembled. With a parting glance at the Judge he left the dock. A murder case had lasted just six minutes.

Larter may not have been legally represented at his trial but local solicitors Mills and Reeve presented a petition for reprieve to the Home Secretary. They received a reply dated 9 February 1909 which said that 'after medical enquiry into the mental condition of the prisoner' the Home Secretary 'has advised His Majesty to respite the capital sentence, with a view to the immediate removal of the convict to the Broadmoor Criminal Lunatic Asylum'. Two doctors appointed by the Home Secretary had agreed that Larter was insane.

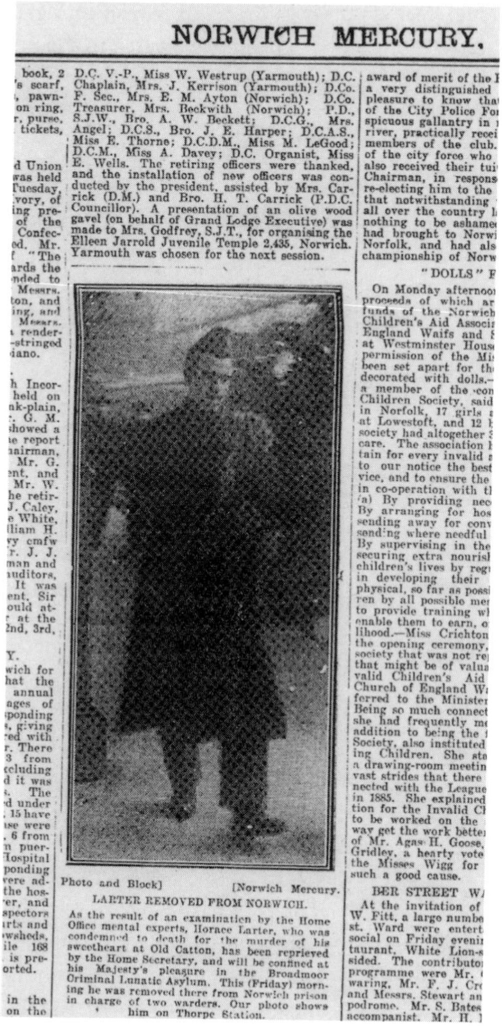
NORWICH MERCURY.

D.C. V.-P., Miss W. Westrup (Yarmouth); D.C. Chaplain, Mrs. J. Kerrison (Yarmouth); D.Co. F. Sec., Mrs. E. M. Ayton (Norwich); D.Co. Treasurer, Mrs. Beckwith (Norwich); P.D., S.J.W., Bro. A. W. Beckett; D.C.G., Mrs. Angel; D.C.S., Bro. J. E. Harper; D.C.A.S., Miss E. Thorne; D.C.D.M., Miss M. LeGood; D.C.M., Miss A. Davey; D.C. Organist, Miss E. Wells. The retiring officers were thanked, and the installation of new officers was conducted by the president, assisted by Mrs. Carrick (D.M.) and Bro. H. T. Carrick (P.D.C. Councillor). A presentation of an olive wood gavel (on behalf of Grand Lodge Executive) was made to Mrs. Godfrey, S.J.T., for organising the Elleen Jarrold Juvenile Temple 2,435, Norwich. Yarmouth was chosen for the next session.

Photo and Block] [Norwich Mercury.

LARTER REMOVED FROM NORWICH.

As the result of an examination by the Home Office mental experts, Horace Larter, who was condemned to death for the murder of his sweetheart at Old Catton, has been reprieved by the Home Secretary, and will be confined at his Majesty's pleasure in the Broadmoor Criminal Lunatic Asylum. This (Friday) morning he was removed there from Norwich prison in charge of two warders. Our photo shows him on Thorpe Station.

Figure 9.8. The Norwich Mercury *took this barely distinguishable photograph of Horace Larter at Thorpe Station. He appears to be dressed in military style and his escort was not close enough to get in the picture.* Archant

On Friday, 12 February, he was placed on a train at Norwich Thorpe Station under prison escort.

The last touching scene in a touching case came from Larter's mother. She wrote to the press thus:

> Dear Sir. Will you be kind enough to let me offer through your paper a mother's most grateful and heartfelt thanks to those kind friends through whose efforts a reprieve has been granted to my unhappy son, Horace Larter.
>
> I remain your grateful and obedient servant,
>
> Elizabeth Larter

Murder creates many victims.

CHAPTER 10

Love and Death:
Third of a Trilogy
The Murder of Eileen Cullen
1951

We continue the pattern of professed love and inexplicable death, moving through improving times and two world wars, the police taking on board forensic evidence from cross contamination by fibres, hairs, and body fluids, identification by fingerprints and matching blood groups, progressing through crime scene photography and steadily improving communications and transport. We arrive at 1951, recalling what became known as the 'Oak Lane murder'.

By 1951 progress had come from other agencies. Post-mortems were conducted in hospitals by qualified pathologists, inquests no longer rivalled committal proceedings and the press had lost the freedom to trample around a 'ghastly spectacle'. Eileen Cullen's murder came upon a more professional, disciplined and respected police force backed by experts, though in 1951 the Norwich City Police were not used to murders because for many years they had not had one. In February of that year they got one, temporarily.

At 8.50 pm on Saturday, 3 February 1951, Station Sergeant Harold Byland answered the telephone in Bethel Street Police Station (a purpose-built police station opened in 1938, replacing the Guildhall) and, with the air of a long serving policeman inured to the wiles, ignorance and hysteria of his public, listened to a young male voice admitting murder. Sergeant Byland was not impressed. Saturday nights produced revellers prone to mischief, plus the usual ration of misguided observers, hoaxers and the odd decoy call. Calling 'murder', much practised by Victorians in assaults and arguments, did not necessarily mean murder; even half a century or more later it might be a clarion call of alarm or excited misperception. His jaundiced view may also have been influenced by the belief that Norwich did not have murders – nobody could remember the last one;

they were history, now occurring outside the city. The Sergeant made a joking aside to colleagues in the Station Office that he had a 'right one' on the line.

The 'right one' was, however, either sincere or a good actor, and he was unusually forthcoming. He gave his position, the roundabout at Catton Grove Road by Woodcock Road, and named his victim, Irene Coleman – although the Sergeant's hearing of the surname was later to be questioned. When asked by the Sergeant he gave his name and address: Dennis Moore of Woodcock Road. These readily supplied details could of course have been false, and indeed Irene Coleman, or any other Irene, had not been murdered, but Dennis Moore really was on the line and he had committed murder.

Sergeant Byland told Moore to stay by the telephone box and sent Detective Constable John McLennan and aide-to–CID Constable Herbert Lines to the given position. Moore waited as instructed and in his words, 'a Black Maria came with two civilians I think were detectives'. Watching the approaching police van he contemplated the events of a day that had promised happiness and delivered tragedy; he had killed the girl he was due to marry in two weeks' time.

Eileen Cullen, twenty-one years of age, and Dennis Moore, twenty-three years of age, had met in June 1950 in Great Yarmouth where the youth of Norwich often enjoyed the pleasures of the sea front, which included eyeing the opposite sex. Eileen had cycled to the seaside resort with her sister Evelyn; Moore had similarly arrived in a group of young men. Eileen and Dennis met, were mutually attracted, and cycled back to Norwich together.

Eileen lived at Buxton Road, a little over a mile from Woodcock Road, and was the eldest of three sisters living with her father, an asphalter, and blind mother. She and her next eldest sister, Evelyn, to whom she was very close, worked at Segger's shoe factory in Botolph Street. Eileen was an attractive young woman with an engaging personality, uncomplicated and happy with life, and clearly attracted to the good looking and presentable young man she had met at Great Yarmouth. She quickly introduced him to her family and he was welcomed at Buxton Road, visiting Eileen there every day. Their relationship blossomed. Dennis Moore was kindly and attentive to Eileen, polite and respectful to her family, and liked by the Cullen family. There was no reason not to like him.

Such was the obvious affection of the young couple for each other Eileen might reasonably have been expecting love to turn into marriage, still the socially required form in those days, a prospect that became reality when she discovered she was pregnant. Moore apologised to her father and said he would marry Eileen as soon as possible. They became engaged on 20 November, her twenty-first birthday, and the wedding date was set for 17 February. Arrangements were made for them to live with Eileen's aunt at nearby Bakers Road and the couple began to accumulate various items for their new home, storing them at Buxton Road and paying jointly for articles they purchased.

Figure 10.1. Eileen Cullen. Evelyn Cousins

Through to Christmas and beyond the engaged couple planned their new life together without any hint of the disaster to come. Even on the fateful day, 3 February, there appeared nothing out of the ordinary; the very opposite for it was the day Eileen went into the city to choose her wedding dress.

The couple met at seven-thirty that Saturday morning at Eileen's home and later had dinner there, following which they went shopping in the city accompanied by Eileen's sister Evelyn as an aid to selecting a wedding dress. In the city Eileen found she had insufficient money and Moore went to Norwich Market to borrow some from his father who kept a fruit and vegetable stall. At ten minutes past four he returned to the stall, at that time in the charge of his brother Gerald and brother-in-law, Victor Sewell, and handed Sewell a ten shilling note saying it was the return of a loan from his father. Moore stood on the footboards at the side of the stall as he returned the money, a position that would later be of some importance.

At half-past five that afternoon Moore and his bride-to-be had tea with the Cullen family at Buxton Road and left at half-past six to visit the doctor supervising Eileen's pregnancy. They were happy and attentive to each other, leaving the house with customary farewells and promises to soon return. Moore told Evelyn they would bring her some chips. Evelyn never got her chips and never saw her sister again.

Doctor Champion saw Eileen and her fiancé together at his surgery in Magdalen Road between 7 and 7.30 pm. They discussed the arrangements for Eileen's forthcoming confinement and the couple left after ten minutes. The doctor later said that both were 'perfectly normal'.

Like so many murder cases what happened next lay within the knowledge of one person. The dead cannot speak, cannot rebut or qualify the version proffered by a person who murders without witnesses. And Eileen died in darkness in a brick shelter situated in a meadow fifty yards from a little used lane called Oak Lane. The shelter had been used as a cattle shed and before that a store for the Home Guard. It was twelve feet eight inches long and eight feet eight inches wide, approached over damp winter grass, unprepossessing outside and cold and uninviting inside. The police measured the distance from the doctor's surgery at 1.3 miles. Without doubt Eileen went there willingly, one of a courting couple seeking privacy and shelter.

Between 7.50 and 8.10 pm Moore entered *The Park House* public house at Catton Grove Road, a few minutes walk from the Oak Lane shelter. A customer and the landlady noted that he was not wearing an overcoat and was generally untidy. He bought ten Kensitas cigarettes and left.

At a time after eight o'clock Moore appeared at his home in Woodcock Road, no more than ten minutes walk from *The Park House,* and asked his mother for a pencil. She asked where Eileen was and he replied, 'She's outside.' He then said, 'Cheerio all, I'll see you when I get home.' He left and, if the evidence is correct, he took a bread knife from the kitchen. His thinking at the time he briefly visited his home remains an enigma. Eileen was already dead. Yet he returned to her body at the Oak Lane shelter, with the bread knife.

He stayed with his dead fiancée in the shelter, possibly only a few minutes, maybe as long as twenty minutes, before leaving to telephone the police, resigned to surrendering. Now he stood at a roundabout contemplating his actions, and the approaching police vehicle.

The police van stopped and Detective Constable McLennan asked, 'Are you Dennis Moore?'

Moore replied, 'Yes, I have strangled my girl Eileen Cullen. I'll show you where she is.'

After being placed in the van he directed the officers to Oak Lane and, pointing to the shelter, said, 'She's in there.'

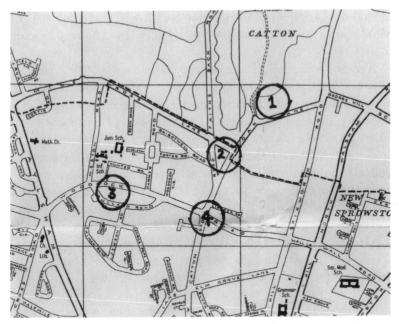

Figure 10.2. A murderer's progress. (1) Scene of the murder, (2) The Park House *public house, (3) The murderer's home, (4) The place where he called and met the police.* Reproduced from 1951 Ordnance Survey map with kind permission of the Ordnance Survey

Walking towards the shelter between the two detectives Moore began to cry and suddenly broke away, running towards the shelter. They caught him at the entrance, holding him back.

A police torch showed that Moore had told the truth. Eileen Cullen lay on her back with a woollen scarf wrapped round her head and over her face. Her head was against a wall, her feet pointing to the entrance. She was wearing an overcoat and a mackintosh lay over her body. Again Moore broke away, throwing himself upon the dead woman crying, 'I love you. I love you.' Again he was pulled back.

Detective Constable McLennan leant by the body and found it was warm. He removed the woollen scarf from the head and found a silk scarf knotted tightly round the neck. He undid the scarf but realised that life was extinct and stepped back to leave the body as near found as possible. Cut marks were visible on the right side of Eileen's neck. Constable Lines went for assistance and Constable McLennan arrested Moore.

Moore said, 'I strangled her with my hands until blood came out of her mouth and I knotted the scarf around her neck, wrapped my scarf around her face, covered her with my coat. I went to the pub and got some cigarettes and then rang the police. I knew it was no good running away.'

A circling police torch revealed other points of interest. A bread knife lay close to Eileen's head, her handbag rested on her lower stomach as if laid there, and at the side of her right knee was a shopping card heavily pencilled in lipstick 'I love her. Goodbye all.' Later, a search of her handbag would reveal an envelope addressed: 'To Eileen, my pretty. From Brian.'

Sergeant Byland soon learned that murder really had been committed and he accordingly alerted all who should respond, and probably some who need not. Superintendent Tester and Inspector Wright of the city force went to the scene, also the Police Surgeon Doctor Lincoln Hurn. Norwich had ended a long run without a murder – or had it? Discussion in Bethel Street Police Station and in a field on a cold February evening quickly concluded that everything pertaining to the murder had occurred in the city, except the murder. Oak Lane was in county territory.

At 10 pm that evening Superintendent Tester and Constable McLennan delivered Moore to the County Police Headquarters at Thorpe Road, handing him over to Detective Sergeant Colin Sidell.

The Superintendent explained that the prisoner had given himself up after strangling his girl friend at Old Catton and Moore said, 'Yes, that's right.'

Detective Superintendent Sydney Kybird of the county force was called out and he went with Sergeant Sidell to Oak Lane to add to the growing number who had peered into the brick shelter. He was now the officer in charge of the case. Murder scenes in the middle twentieth century were more tightly controlled and more comprehensively investigated than those of previous years, but a greater procession of officialdom to and from the body came from experts in forensic evidence, fingerprint retrieval and photography, with assistants, plus the Police Surgeon and a pathologist examining the body *in situ* before conducting his post-mortem in a mortuary. In this case policemen from two forces trudged across a field to where Eileen Cullen lay. But no longer would the press and public obtain a viewing.

Doctor Hurn examined the body at 10.20 pm and certified death, opining that it had occurred one or two hours previously. At eleven-thirty Superintendent Kybird, Sergeant Sidell and Detective Constable Kimpton viewed the body, the latter a 'scenes of crime' officer trained in forensic and fingerprint retrieval and photography. He would later attend

Figures 10.3 & 10.4. These police photographs were taken the following morning when Eileen Cullen still lay in the brick shelter. 10.3 shows her last walk, coming from the distance and turning left into the field, and 10.4 shows the path well-trodden by police and doctors to the shelter. Norfolk Constabulary & National Archives

the post-mortem with the investigating officers and photograph all relevant marks and injuries.

The body was guarded overnight and visited by pathologist Doctor David Fulton from Nottingham at eleven-thirty the next morning. Normal practice would see the body removed under supervision of the pathologist, assisted by the scenes of crime officer and the police officer designated to be 'exhibits officer'.

Doctor Fulton conducted his post-mortem at the Norfolk and Norwich Hospital and reported, as expected, that death had been due to asphyxia caused by a ligature tied tightly around the neck. He also reported other injuries: extensive bruising round the right eye, a large bruise at the back of the head, 'a number of superficial transverse cuts in the skin of the neck' and a 'superficial abrasion under the left ear'. He found a pregnancy of approximately four months.

Doctor Fulton was of the opinion the bread knife could have caused the marks on Eileen's neck. He did not give an opinion as to the cause of the other injuries.

A freely confessing murderer does not mean a truthful one. Confusion, shock or simply an attempt to dilute the consequences of the killing may result in a distorted explanation or simply no explanation at all for given circumstances. Dennis Moore made two statements under caution, the one in answer to the charge of murder saying that he understood the charge, finishing 'I'm sorry I've done this and hope I've not caused too much worry on either of our parents,' the other a more lengthy and detailed document that went into how he met Eileen, intended to marry her and killed her.

Moore's main statement described the events of 3 February leading up to the visit to Doctor Champion's surgery following which they walked to Oak Lane quarrelling as they went. They went into the brick shelter and kissed and cuddled and he wanted sex and she didn't, he said. The next part of his statement requires exactness.

> I put my arms round her and squeezed her to me tightly, the next thing I realised she had fallen to the floor and her mouth was all bleeding. I then realised I had hold of her throat and I just couldn't leave go. After that I took her scarf, put two knots in it and tied it round her neck very tight. I then took my own scarf off and wrapped it round her mouth, I also took my rain mack off and laid over her and walked up to *The Park House* to get some cigarettes, then to the telephone kiosk and dialled 999 from the box at the bottom of Woodcock Road.

The attentive reader will have noticed the intervening visit to his home is not mentioned. Later in the statement, obviously prompted by earlier police questioning, he goes back to the shelter in a renewed account of what happened.

Tonight was the first time I have ever been in that shed. When I realised what I had done I sat in the porchway of the shed and took her lipstick out of her handbag and I wrote with her lipstick "I LOVE HER – GOODBYE". I felt like running away but I thought twice and came for the police, because I thought it would be better for me. I never carry a knife about with me, but the knife lying on the table looks like my mother's bread knife, I don't remember taking it to the shed. We had got over our tiff when this happened. I can't remember putting my hands round her throat, all I know is I had them tightly round her throat when she fell to the floor. I couldn't leave go. I loved her too much, I wouldn't have hurt her, not for anything in the world.

Some of these words are familiar to other cases of death from professed love. His statement finished:

That's all except my tie there. I don't remember taking it off. I have been wearing it all day.

So the tie (found at the scene) and the bread knife remained enigmas, ancillary to Eileen's death from her own silk scarf. Whether he had used or planned to use the tie is not known but the bread knife had without doubt been used, albeit without conviction. The key to Moore's state of mind would be where the bread knife came from and when.

The envelope from 'Brian' proved to be a red herring. Evelyn had a similar one. The author was a twelve-year-old boy living in Buxton Road and admiring the sisters from afar.

Procedural progress in the twentieth century saw the inquest and formal committal to trial implemented without the duplicity of previous legal administrations, though inquests still favoured public houses. Eileen Cullen's inquest began in *The Woodman* at Catton. She was laid to rest on 10 February at Earlham Cemetery attended by a large crowd of mourners. Segger's shoe factory shut down to allow all the staff to attend the funeral of this popular young woman.

Figure 10.5. The note written in lipstick, found near the body.
Norfolk Constabulary & National Archives

Figure 10.6. The envelope found in Eileen's handbag – a red herring. Norfolk Constabulary & National Archives

At the remand hearing at the Shirehall Moore appeared in a crumpled pullover, without collar or tie, and hailed his father in the Court. He answered the charge with 'Correct' though whether that meant he approved of the wording or was guilty of its allegation is not known. For sure he would not plead 'Guilty' at his trial. His life was at stake. Capital punishment still remained the punishment for murder.

Thursday, 31 May 1951 and he appeared before Mr Justice Parker, represented by Mr Alpe. John Flowers KC, prosecuted for the Crown. A plea of 'Not Guilty' was entered and the defence case emerged as an acceptance of the killing (difficult to argue otherwise) but performed whilst 'labouring under a defect of reasoning'. Simply put, the defence said Moore did not know what he doing because of temporary insanity and therefore his responsibility was diminished – a defence that within a few years would be formalised by statute and is consequently more familiar today. The prosecution said otherwise: that he knew exactly what he was doing and had the malice aforethought necessary for murder. (Wilful was no longer bandied around quite so freely – all murders are wilful by definition.)

The prosecution sought to prove that the bread knife, identified as coming from Moore's home, had on the day of the murder come from his father's fruit and vegetable stall on Norwich Market, appropriated by Moore when he returned the ten shillings. Whilst the Moore family agreed that a bread knife from the family home sometimes found itself on the stall for the purpose of cleaning leeks, and there was some discrepancy between them whether it had been there on 3 February, evidence at the trial placed it in the kitchen at Woodcock Road at about 7.30 pm. This argument was crucial for if Moore had taken it from the stall he must have had some determination long before he killed Eileen. Eventually, the prosecution accepted that the knife had not been taken from the stall by Moore, Mr Flowers saying he had only made that suggestion in accordance with the depositions. The defence had scored a victory concerning the bread knife but it was a brief success.

Sergeant Byland in the witness box admitted that he might have misheard the name of the victim given by Moore in his telephone call. Mr Flowers suggested that the name given had been 'Irene Hambling', not Irene Coleman. In any event there was agreement that it had not been Eileen Cullen.

The neutral observer wondering about Irene Hambling was soon enlightened. The prosecution called her as a witness and her evidence came as a bombshell. She had been Dennis Moore's girlfriend from April 1949 to April 1950 and they had parted company after she had found she was pregnant and her father had become extremely angry. It got worse. She and Moore had quarrelled on a towpath and he had tried to strangle her, she said. She now lived in London.

The defence might have said that Moore using an ex-girlfriend's name when reporting the murder truly showed an aberration of the mind, but the prosecution were intent on showing psychopathic tendencies and they called a witness to reveal that Moore had engaged in a wrestling match during his National Service at Colchester and had tried to strangle his opponent.

Mr Flowers in summing up to the jury for the prosecution said he had no intention of misleading them over the bread knife but Moore's advances to Eileen had been repellent and he had formed an 'overpowering rage'. He said, 'In this imperfect world many people had killed the person they loved in passion' and such an act was 'miles and miles away from insanity'.

Mr Alpe in his defence speech to the jury said that if the bread knife had been taken from the market stall it meant premeditation of 'this dreadful and horrible act' but that had not been the case, now agreed by the prosecution. He referred to the knotted scarf used to kill Eileen and said that related to a murder Moore had seen at the cinema. He rhetorically asked 'Was this the act of a man's sound mind towards the woman he loved?'

The Judge summed up without obviously taking sides (defending lawyers would seize on any bias for consideration by the Appeal Court) and the jury retired. They returned after fifty minutes and found the prisoner 'Guilty'. The Judge said he 'entirely agreed with the verdict' and without much preamble sentenced Moore to death.

Moore's defence of temporary insanity was taken to the Appeal Court in company with the appeal of Alfred Reynolds, aged twenty-five years, of Dereham, also convicted of strangling his girlfriend. Both appeals were dismissed within ten minutes, Lord Goddard observing that there was no reason for the Appeal Court 'interfering in any shape or form'.

A vigorously conducted petition, at one point insensitively taken to Segger's shoe factory, failed to impress the Home Secretary. There was no reprieve and at 8 am on Thursday, 19 July 1951 Dennis Moore and Alfred Reynolds were simultaneously hanged at Norwich Prison. The prison bell tolled its melancholy message across Mousehold Heath and was heard in Buxton Road.

Moore and Reynolds were the last to suffer the ultimate punishment in Norwich and they died in times of growing opposition to the death penalty. As far back as 1854 there had been a public meeting opposing executions. Nearly one hundred years later, in 1948, the House of Commons voted to abolish the death penalty for a five year trial period, only to be thwarted by the House of Lords; and the Abolition Bill of 1956 also floundered in the House of Lords. The 1957 Homicide Act brought in categories of murder to receive the death penalty and through its provisions Moore and Reynolds would have lived and, as presumed sane men, eventually been released; and probably be with us today. They found a place in history and the inquest verdict on these two men was recorded in Norwich for the last time: 'hanging pursuant to the execution of the law.'

The last judicial hanging in Great Britain took place in 1964 and the death penalty for murder was finally abolished in 1965. The sanctity of life had been preserved, though there could of course be no reprieve for Eileen Cullen, or Nellie Howard, or Jennie Plunkett.

Epilogue

On 1 January 1968 a new police administration erased the border of the city and county forces, a territorial difference much in evidence in this book. Future Norwich murders fell inside the new City Division, their investigation allied to a new force headquarters at Martineau Lane (opposite where Martha Sheward was partly found). And the twenty-first century saw yet another new police headquarters – another place known to this book: Wymondham!

The incidence of murders in Norwich had varied considerably over two centuries and a long spell without the ultimate crime looked set to continue to the end of the Norwich City Police, scheduled for midnight, 31 December 1967. In the late evening of Saturday, 30 December 1967, a murder was reported.

Manuel Gomez, a watch repairer on Norwich Market, died on the pavement in Stevenson Road, battered to death with a 'road rammer' after an argument had overflowed from a nearby house. Donald MacLennan, a general dealer, was charged with murder by the city police, a force that within hours would be renamed and integrated into a new force. MacLennan said he was drunk and couldn't remember anything that took place. A jury found him 'Not Guilty' of murder but 'Guilty' of manslaughter, reaching this verdict by a 10–2 majority: another innovation never envisaged by those pioneer policemen.

The latter part of the twentieth century saw investigative techniques moulded into Incident Room systems. National training came through New Scotland Yard and the Police College, the Home Office's love of acronyms exampled by MIRIAM ('Major Incident Room Index and Action Management') and HOLMES (Home Office Large Major Enquiry System). HOLMES survives today, refined and constantly improving, inspired by computer technology. How the police of yesteryear would have marvelled. And what would they have made of the linking of victim and murderer by a magic formula known as DNA?

During the accelerating progress of the latter part of the twentieth century several murders occurred in Norwich but this book is not encyclopaedic and ends, as introduced, with the Norwich City Police, or nearly so, for murder knows no bounds. No person or place is sacred, including hospitals and prisons. In December 1875, a male patient in the Norfolk and Norwich Hospital ran amok in the children's ward and murdered four boys aged between nine and fourteen years and, outside our time frame, in 1980, murder was committed inside Norwich Prison. (There would be another there before the end of the century.)

The 1980 murder demonstrates the utter tragedy of wilfully taking a life. A nineteen-year-old timid and inadequate young man, detained for theft from a linen line, volunteered a confession to rape, finding some sense of importance in the attention he then received. Magistrates remanded him to Norwich Prison. Detectives, uneasy over his confession, interviewed him in prison and, satisfied that he was innocent of rape, arranged for him to be brought before the Magistrates to withdraw the charge. That night a hardened London criminal strangled him in the hospital dormitory for no other reason than he was available. A young innocent man had been in the wrong place, at the wrong time. All the victims in this book were available and innocent, and in the wrong place at the wrong time.

Bibliography

Norwich City Police Watch Committee Minutes

Chief Constable Reports to Norfolk Police Authority

Newspapers reports of: *Norfolk Chronicle & Norwich Gazette*, *Norwich Mercury*, *Norfolk News*, *Norfolk Daily Standard*, *Eastern Daily Press* and *Eastern Evening News*

National Archives: depositions, exhibits, Assize records etc.

Norfolk Heritage Centre reports, records etc.

Norfolk Record Office reports, documents etc.

Norfolk Constabulary and Police Archive reports, records etc.

Norfolk Annals by Charles Mackie

A History of Norwich by Frank Meeres

Norwich in the Nineteenth Century by Christopher Barringer

Disappearing Norwich and *Rambles in Old Norwich* by George Plunkett

Index